Transforming
Teacher
Unions

Fighting
for
Better Schools
and
Social Justice

edited by

Bob Peterson

and

Michael Charney

RETHINKING SCHOOLS
MILWAUKEE, WISCONSIN

Rethinking Schools, Ltd. is a nonprofit educational publisher of books, booklets, and a quarterly
journal on school reform, with a focus on issues of equity and social justice.

To request additional copies of this book or a catalog of other publications,
or to subscribe to the *Rethinking Schools* journal, contact:

Rethinking Schools
1001 East Keefe Ave
Milwaukee, Wisconsin 53212
(toll-free 1-800-669-4192)
www.rethinkingschools.org

Transforming Teacher Unions: Fighting for Better Schools and Social Justice
© 1999, Rethinking Schools, Ltd.

Cover photograph (girl) by Jean-Claude LeJeune. Background image by Michael Poche, courtesy AP/Wide World Photos. Used by permission.

Book design by Maclean & Tuminelly, Minneapolis

Special thanks to the following people who helped with this book: Peter Arum, Bill Bigelow, Joanna Dupuis, Stan Karp, Robert Lowe, Philip Martin, Barbara Miner, Joel Shapiro, Mark Simon, Adam Urbanski, and all the writers and interviewees who contributed their time and efforts. Thanks also to the Joyce Foundation of Chicago for their support of this project.

ISBN # 0-942961-24-2. Manufactured in the U.S.A.   42

Library of Congress Cataloging-in-Publication Data

Transforming teacher unions : fighting for better schools and social justice /
edited by Bob Peterson and Michael Charney.
p.   cm.
Includes bibliographical references.
ISBN 0-942961-24-2 (pbk. : alk. paper)
1. Teachers' unions—United States. 2. Teachers' unions—Canada.
I. Peterson, Bob. II. Charney, Michael.
LB2844.53.U6T73   1999
331.88'113711'0973—dc21

399-30500
CIP

Table of Contents

Introduction

THE MERE MENTION OF "TEACHER UNIONS" ELICITS impassioned responses. Some claim that teacher unions are the major obstacle to school reform. Others find little fault. Still others note that in some areas, union locals have been a driving force in reform.

Despite these differing perspectives, there is one area of agreement. Teacher unions are one of the most powerful forces in education. The direction they take will shape not only their own future but that of public education and, potentially, that of society at large.

In order to meet the challenges of today and tomorrow, we believe that teacher unions must embark on a new path. Too often, teacher unions — like public education itself — have had a mixed record on fighting for an equitable and quality education for all children. Too often, they have been accomplices in maintaining an unsatisfactory status quo.

This doesn't have to be the case. We believe the unions can and must embrace a new vision, one we define as social justice unionism. Underlying this vision is a commitment to equity and excellence in education for all children. Already, a number of activists and leaders have taken steps to define and implement aspects of this vision of social justice unionism. We believe it has three main components:

• **Defending public education and the rights of teachers.** Teacher unions must continue to militantly defend the very concept of public education, uphold the rights of teachers as workers, and demand improved conditions of teaching and learning.

• **Strong emphasis on professionalism.** Teacher unions must take responsibility for the quality of the teacher corps. Teacher mentoring, staff development, and high quality teaching must be ever-present issues, ensuring that all children are learning and that all teachers are quality teachers.

• **Commitment to children and community.** Teacher unions must build a strategic alliance with parents and communities in which all are equal partners in fighting for what is best for children in schools and in society. Teacher unions must forthrightly address the issues of race that dominate both our schools and our social and political institutions.

Integral to social justice unionism is the question of union democracy and increased rank-and-file participation. Too often teachers don't view themselves as an integral part of their union, seeing "the union" as only the small group in leadership or the paid staff. Certain practices in some locals — ranging from questionable election procedures to boring, top-down meetings — discourage teachers from full participation.

In addition, there has been a historic divide between those who commit themselves to union activities and those who commit themselves to improving teaching practices by starting innovative schools, leading district curriculum committees, being active in the community, or participating in state and national professional organizations. Clearly, teacher unions must devise better ways of bridging that divide and involving such experienced teachers.

A Powerful Force

Teacher unions are clearly under attack and, in key areas, on the defensive. Yet they remain a powerful force. There are over 2.6 million elementary and secondary teachers in the public schools, and more than 85% are organized into either the National Education Association (NEA) or the American Federation of Teachers (AFT).

The unions' power is not just based on numbers. The heart of our education system lies in the relationship between teacher and student. Further, teachers intimately understand the difficult conditions facing our nation's children. Teachers must be recognized as

Thousands of Ontario teachers demonstrate at the Ontario Legislature in Toronto, Canada, on Oct. 27, 1997, in the largest teachers' strike in North American history. The main issue was the provincial government's attempt to take over policy-making powers held by local school boards.

essential resources in developing reform initiatives that will really work.

Teacher unions (in most states) also have collective bargaining agreements as a source of power. Such agreements can be a way to institutionalize reforms that improve public education and classroom conditions — for example, through limits on class size. The agreements can also act as a force for stability, especially when school boards are marked by political infighting and superintendents suffer from the revolving-door syndrome. Critics, of course, view union contracts as obstacles to reform, citing rigidity in areas such as staffing and evaluation. The best way for unionists to counter such criticisms is to defend the right to bargain collectively while simultaneously showing flexibility and using negotiations to foster school improvement.

Finally, teacher unions have power in the legislative arena, at the local, state, and national level. This power has been used not only to support specific legislation but also to elect candidates who support public education. Proponents of a combined AFT/NEA point out that such an organization would have a minimum of 1,200 members in each congressional district in the nation — which could significantly improve the unions' political power.

The key question facing the teacher unions is how they will use their power.

Teacher unions have excelled in furthering the economic aims and job security of teachers. They also have a history of concern with professional issues such as teacher training and adequate resources. Further, in different locations and in different times, teachers unions have been important supporters of progressive social policies, for instance supporting the civil rights movement and, more recently, supporting health care reform.

On the other hand, teacher unions have sometimes pursued policies that are not in the best interests of the children teachers teach. This has been particularly true when teachers' interests have conflicted with the demands of communities of color in urban areas. Clearly, teacher unions (which are predominantly white) must be more sensitive to issues of race — internally among members, in their relations with parents and communities, and in fostering anti-racist policies and curricula within the schools. Despite their predominantly white character, in many cities teacher unions are still one of the more integrated organizations around and thus have the potential to become a positive force rooted in the community.

In This Book

The analyses and articles in this book highlight a vision of teacher unionism that builds on and yet transcends the past. We begin with an article explaining in detail the vision of social justice unionism. In the same "Overview" section, there's a perspective on a "New Vision of Schooling" that imagines what schooling could be like under different conditions. Elsewhere in this collection, you will find statements by national leaders of the NEA and AFT, interviews with local leaders, and articles on innovative reforms pushed by local affiliates.

As we pulled together this book, we became acutely aware that there are very few examples of teacher-union practices focused on social justice. Most of the "reports from the field" we've included are exemplary examples of "professional" unionism. They focus primarily on improving the quality of the teaching profession, and only secondarily, or not at all, on the inequities in schools and society.

A few of the articles in our collection clearly move into the realm of social justice unionism. These include some of the turn-of-the-century activities of the Chicago AFT under Margaret Haley's leadership, the depression-era work done in Harlem by the Teachers Union (AFT #5), and the ongoing work by the British Columbia Teachers' Federation based on their Program Against Racism. We hope that in the next few years, we can report in the pages of *Rethinking Schools* more examples of bold social justice teacher-union practices.

Don't get us wrong. We think unions should be both professional and social justice in orientation. What we've come to understand, however, is that no matter how successful any set of professional reforms may be, they will fall short of ensuring that "all children can learn" unless the social inequalities that face our children are also overcome. Schools can do more and do better, but they can't do it all. And if we proclaim that any one set of professional reforms or standards or even increased school funding will ensure that all our children learn, we are setting ourselves up for failure — and ultimately opening our unions and public education to attack by the right.

That's why social justice unionism must include the professional reforms outlined in these pages but also much more — a commitment to a more inclusive and equitable vision of society. Thus we have included the interview with historian Howard Zinn and articles linking the defense of public education to the need for a democratic movement that makes government accountable to the interests of all its citizens.

Near the end is a listing of additional resources and questions that might help frame discussion circles around these topics. We encourage readers to let us know what they think about these articles and suggest that you subscribe to *Rethinking Schools* as one way to monitor and participate in an ongoing discussion of these important issues.

The conversations in this book focus on schools. But ultimately, the discussion is about what kind of society we want to create. We believe that teachers can make a significant contribution to building a social movement that advances both our interests as education workers and our broader interests as democratic citizens. We can build schools where all children reach their true potential. We can forge ties with parents and community groups to take up issues of school reform and social change. We can insist that our unions foster broader participation by all members and provide leadership in professional and social justice issues. If we do these things, together, we will all benefit. **TU**

— *Bob Peterson & Michael Charney*
June 1999

Overview

Survival and Justice: Rethinking Teacher Union Strategy

BY BOB PETERSON

NEVER IN THE HISTORY OF OUR NATION HAVE PUBLIC schools been under such relentless attack. Never in the history of teacher unionism has there been a greater urgency to rethink strategy.

To meet these challenges, our public schools and our teacher unions should set two key goals: survival and justice. Furthermore, these goals are inextricably linked. Our system of public education and our teacher unions will not survive unless they more forthrightly address issues of social justice.

To put the matter succinctly, those who understand the vital importance of a system of public education must simultaneously defend and transform our public schools so that they equitably serve all students. And those who understand the vital role of teacher unions must simultaneously defend members' rights while building a new vision of teacher unionism.

In recent years, there has been growing attention to these complicated questions. In particular, an increas-

> *Social justice unionism views itself as part of a broader movement for social progress rather than merely focused on narrow self interest.*
> *It calls for participatory union membership, education reform to serve all children, collaboration with community organizations, and a concern for broader issues of equity.*

ing number of teacher unionists understand the need to move beyond a traditional industrial approach and recognize that teachers are also professionals responsible for building better schools. Thus they advocate what has been called "professional unionism." Within this professional unionism trend, some have advocated "social justice unionism." Simply put, this third approach builds on the best of industrial unionism, embraces essential concepts of professional unionism, and adds a vision of social justice. This social justice perspective is grounded in the need to advocate for all students which in turn leads directly to confronting issues of race and class. This perspective informs a range of topics — from union democracy to the purpose of schooling, from teachers' relationships with students, parents, and community to the need to radically restructure society.

I believe a significant number of teacher union-

KATHY SLOANE

- Had so much respect in the community that when a parent had a problem in a school, the parent would not only talk to the principal and their child's teacher, but to the union rep as well.

- Operated a teachers' development center where teachers taught teachers and earned university credit for participation.

- Ran a mentoring program where every new teacher received intensive help from a mentor who had enough time to help new teachers.

- Had a community outreach program in which union members regularly spoke at churches, community groups, sororities, and fraternities in order to garner support for public education.

- Was racially diverse and reflected the composition of the student body.

- Self-monitored its members so that all teachers were of high quality.

ists will be drawn to a social justice perspective, if for no other reason than it is in teachers' long-term self-interest. What in the past may have been dismissed as the luxury of "doing the right thing" is now a matter of necessity. If teacher unions are to survive, they must take responsibility for building better and more equitable schools. But better and more equitable schools will not be possible unless there is increased attention to providing opportunities for all students and their families within society at large. Our schools, in the long run, will only be as healthy and vibrant as the communities they serve.

In this essay, I will lay out the current political context, particularly as it relates to education. I will then look at the key components of the three strands of teacher unionism (industrial, professional, and social justice). Finally, I will end with a look at two top issues in education — teacher accountability and the racial dynamics of schooling — and how the different models address these issues.

Political Context

Efforts to rethink teacher-union strategy take place within a complicated political context, especially the public education "crisis" and the conservative and anti-union backlash. There are also the specific peculiarities of teachers as public service workers.

The public education "crisis" operates on two parallel tracks. On the one hand, there is a very real crisis facing our public schools. On the other hand, the crisis, especially as it is portrayed in the media, is manufactured as part of a broader political move to privatize and defund our public education system.

Anyone involved in education knows that there is a crisis in schooling — and that this crisis is centered on issues of equity. It's not that this country does not know how to educate children, but that we do so unequally. It's not that this country doesn't have good schools, but that they are clustered in affluent communities. It's not that this country refuses to spend money on children, but that it is disproportionately showered on already privileged children. As a result, there are an increasing number of

under-funded, unequal, and segregated school systems that are doing an admittedly inadequate job of educating their students. This has a particularly negative effect on low-income students in urban areas.

But the crisis that is portrayed in the media is of a different nature. The media crisis rarely talks of inequitable funding, of widely disparate communities with widely disparate resources, of this country's growing gap between the haves and the have-nots. Instead, this media crisis cuts a broader swath and acts as if public schools cannot do anything right and that teacher unions are the enemies of education.

This is where the crisis in education intersects with the conservative and anti-union political milieu. The media's portrayal is based in part on the journalistic approach that "good news is not news" — in other words, only bad news and controversy are worthy of a story. But it is also the result of groundwork by the conservative movement. For years, a well-funded network of right-wing foundations, think tanks, and legal agencies have coordinated their attacks on public schools as part of a broader goal. Their purpose is not to resolve the real crisis in education, the crisis of inequality. Rather, their goal is to reduce public oversight and responsibility for our schools and instead make schools beholden to the rules of the marketplace. As educational consultant Ann Bastian has noted, "Privatizing public education is the centerpiece, the grand prize, of the right wing's overall agenda to dismantle social entitlements and government responsibility for social needs."

Attacking public schools has served another political purpose for conservatives. Low-income African Americans and Latinos are those who have been most dis-served by our public schools. Conservatives have focused on winning over Latinos and African Americans in order to both build support for their voucher and privatization initiatives and to win over constituencies that have traditionally been viewed as part of the Democratic Party base.

Conservatives also recognize the power of the teacher unions — as a check on private and corporate power, as major supporters of the Democratic Party, and as bulwarks of support for progressive national policies ranging from health care, to gay rights, to bilingual education, to affirmative action. Thus they have used their attacks on public education as a way to erode the power of teacher unions.

Unfortunately, these attacks on teacher unions are coming at a time when the labor movement as a whole is on the defensive and progressive social movements are on the decline.

Both the American Federation of Teachers (AFT) and National Education Association (NEA) rose to national prominence in the mid 1960s and early 1970s at the time of a more robust labor movement and a strong civil rights movement. In comparison, the current attacks against teacher unions come in the midst of a 30-year decline in the U.S. labor movement and a waning of many social movements, in particular the modern civil rights movement. Overall, union member-ship has fallen from about 31% of the labor force in 1970 to just under 14% in 1998, even though levels of public service (and teacher) union membership have risen.

The diminished power of the civil rights movement is reflected in the rollbacks of affirmative action, social welfare, and other equity-enhancing programs. One telling indication of the changing times: President Johnson launched a War on Poverty; Presi-dent Clinton capitulated to the conservative war on welfare.

This is the broad political context in which teacher unions operate. But there are added complexities, because teacher unions represent public service workers. This leads to three particular problems.

Public Service Workers

First, as public sector workers, teachers are paid through taxes which come dispropor-tionately from working people. Therefore, the needs of schools and teachers are often pitted against the stretched budgets of poor and working taxpayers. Conservative and business interests have successfully manipu-lated this contradiction to justify decreased funding of public schools, especially in urban

JEAN-CLAUDE LEJEUNE

areas.

Second, teachers do not produce tangible gadgets such as cars, wrenches, or lawnmowers. The "product" of teachers' work is the education of children. Autoworkers can go on strike and demand that, as human beings, their needs take precedence over producing mere steel and chrome. But if teachers are seen as placing their needs above the needs of students, they understandably risk jeopardizing public support.

Third, the issues of race and institutional inequality complicate the role of teachers. The unequal character of schooling mani-fests itself in many ways — in segregated school districts, the racial gap in achieve-ment, and funding inequities. Race is also an issue when looking at questions such as the predominantly white composition of the teaching force and the lack of a quality multicultural curriculum in most schools. Thus schools often become a focal point for racial tensions.

Race is at the heart of so many issues confronting our society — poverty, health care, housing segregation, unemployment, to name a few. Schools, despite their inequities, remain the main social institution commit-ted to a vision of equality. As such, schools are expected to solve the problems of racial inequality without a complementary effort in other parts of society.

IMAGINE IF YOUR TEACHERS UNION...

- Played a role in deter-mining who enters the teaching profession.

- Had a program against racism and prejudice, with a place teachers could turn to for staff development, curricular materials, and support.

- Worked in an on-going alliance with commu-nity, parent, and labor groups on a range of social policies.

- Held membership meetings that were lively exchanges on important educational and social issues, rather than top-down assemblies of leader-ship speeches and reports.

New Strategies for a New Time

The precarious position of teacher unions has sparked debates on strategy within both the NEA and AFT. NEA President Bob Chase has called for a "new unionism." AFT President Sandra Feldman has called on teachers to take more professional responsibility for school success and failure. (See pp. 107 and 111.)

Delegates at state and national conventions have hotly debated these issues. Many questions have been posed: How can teacher unions best defend public schools? How can unions ensure that teachers are treated more professionally? How can unions better serve the needs of all students while defending the interests of teachers?

Such debates are not new, nor are they unique to teacher unions. Historically, union leaders have had to weigh their own members' interests against the interests of the broader working class. (See article, page 20, on how some unions in the past excluded women and people of color.)

There are also contemporary examples. In private industry, unions may support ecologically questionable construction projects or needless government "defense" programs, both of which benefit relatively few workers at the expense of many. Among public-sector workers, including teachers, a union's focus on worker protection may come at the expense of the quality of the service provided to the broader public.

Teacher unions (and many other unions, for that matter) need to rethink their strategies and move beyond narrow trade-union protectionism. Otherwise, they will remain isolated from their natural allies. Conservatives will take advantage of such isolation to help destroy not only teacher unions but public schools.

In looking at these complicated questions, I have found it helpful to look at three different models of teacher unionism: "industrial-style," "professional," and "social justice." I would like to add an important caveat, however. These are somewhat arbitrary distinctions, most useful in helping to frame discussion. In practice, the models are rarely so purely implemented and often overlap, blending into one another depending on circumstances.

The essential components of each approach are:

• The industrial unionism model focuses on defending the working conditions and rights of teachers.

• The professional model incorporates yet moves beyond an industrial model and suggests that unions also play a leading role in professional issues such as teacher accountability and quality of school programs. NEA President Chase's call for "new unionism" has been most identified with this professional model.

• The social justice model embraces concepts of industrial and professional unionism, but also is linked to a tradition that views unions as part of a broader movement for social progress. It calls for participatory union membership; education reform focused on serving all children, with special attention to collaboration with parents and community organizations; and a concern for broader issues of equity throughout society.

Industrial Unionism

It would be foolhardy not to recognize the strengths of the industrial unionism model. Indeed, it is an unfortunate commentary that many current teachers are unaware of the history of teacher unionism.

Tens of thousands of new teachers are replacing retiring veterans who were

part of the militant teacher struggles of the 1960s and 1970s. The new teachers have grown up in an era when "free-market" ideology and individual entrepreneurship have reigned supreme. Their teacher education programs have taught them next to nothing about what it took to win decent working conditions for teachers.

New teachers need to understand that a key strength of teacher unionism has been organizing and winning the right to collectively bargain. Paying teachers respectable wages and benefits and defending their academic and procedural rights can contribute to the overall quality of education. While some teachers, particularly in the NEA, don't wish to admit it, this strength depends on teachers having a "trade-union consciousness" that recognizes that teachers, like other working people, sell their labor power in order to survive and need protection from management.

For instance, Marjorie Murphy writes in her book *Blackboard Unions: The AFT and the NEA 1900 - 1980* of numerous cases of arbitrary dismissal of teachers. The reasons ranged from being married (for women), to being members of integrated organizations (in the South), to being, or accused of being, a communist (particularly in New York). More recent examples include teachers who have been disciplined for their sexual orientation or their political activism. With the growing strength of the religious right and its increasingly successful efforts to influence school boards, teachers must be vigilant in defending basic rights of academic freedom and due process.

Wages, working conditions, and teacher rights were the main focuses of the industrial-style teacher unionism that became dominant in the late 1960s and early 1970s. The AFT initially was more willing to go on strike and was more successful in convincing teachers from large cities to join its union. This helped propel the NEA toward a more militant industrial-union model. For the NEA, this meant a significant change; until the mid-1960s, its national leadership was dominated by superintendents and administrators who tended not to see teachers as "workers" in the traditional union sense of the word.

By the late 1960s and early 1970s, both the AFT and NEA were conducting strikes to ensure better wages, benefits, and pensions, as well as job protection from dictatorial principals and school boards. This forced most school districts in the country to bargain collectively (with the South being the notable exception). The two unions grew in size and strength; through their collective bargaining agreements, they helped determine a wide range of policy. Relationships with local school authorities tended to be contentious and adversarial. Unions put a priority on protecting the rights of teachers, while district administrators focused on protecting their bureaucratic power and procedures. The best interests of children were often slighted.

There are several crucial shortcomings to the industrial approach. Often, it has lead teacher unions to negotiate contracts that rarely address broader educational and professional issues. To be fair, this is not just because of narrow attitudes on the part of union leaders, but also because of restrictive state laws and management's desires to dominate school operations. These factors engender a "serve the contract" mentality that narrowly focuses on individual members' concerns rather than larger professional or social issues.

To insist that our schools ensure the success of all students is important for the sake of equity and for basic job satisfaction — when we go home at night we want to know that we've been successful.

Professional Unionism

Both at grassroots and national levels, there has been increasing uncomfortableness with the constraints of the industrial union approach. As a result, there have been calls for "professional unionism" — a phrase used extensively by professors Charles Kerchner and Julia Koppich in their book, *A Union of Professionals: Labor Relations and Educational Reform,* (see article on page 123).

The most successful advocates of professional unionism have kept, yet moved beyond, the strengths of the industrial model. In particular, several pioneering locals have maintained a focus on defending teachers' economic and social well-being, while at the same time they have promoted innovative reforms that speak to the interests of students. These locals include the Rochester Teachers Association led by Adam Urbanski, the Columbus Education Association led by John Grossman, and the Cincinnati Federation of Teachers led by Tom Mooney (see articles, p. 31 and p. 51). (Ironically, although the AFT traditionally has been viewed as the more militant industrial-type union, and the NEA associated with a more "professional" approach, it has been AFT locals that have tended to be pioneers in radical innovations such as peer review and career ladders.)

In addition to innovative local leaders, the move toward a professional model of unionism has been promoted by a variety of national leaders — mostly significantly the NEA's Chase and the AFT's Feldman. But it also includes members of the Teacher Union Reform Network (TURN), a grouping of 21 AFT and NEA local presidents. (See article, page 22.)

The hallmarks of professional unionism are:

• Teachers are professionals who uphold high teaching standards.

• Teachers understand the interdependency of teachers with the local school authorities; collaboration, not confrontation, is the preferred approach.

• Teachers, and not just management, are responsible for ensuring that all students are learning and that all teachers are quality teachers. Quality teaching is the main way to ensure equity for all students.

The clearest articulation of professional unionism was in a February 1997 speech by the NEA's Chase, shortly after he became president. (See excerpts, page 107.)

"Simply put, in the decade ahead we must revitalize our public schools from within or they will be dismantled from without," Chase said. "... The fact is that while NEA does not control curriculum, set funding levels, or hire and fire, we cannot go on denying responsibility for school quality. ...

"Our new directions are clear: putting issues of school quality front and center at the bargaining table, collaborating actively with management on an agenda of school reform, involving teachers and other school employees in organizing their schools for excellence."

Social Justice Unionism

Some have advocated a new vision of unionism that would go beyond professional concerns and ground itself in a commitment to social justice. The clearest articulation of this perspective was in the document "Social Justice Unionism: A Working Draft." (See page 128.) The document was written in the summer of 1994 during a "union institute" sponsored by the National Coalition of Education Activists and attended by activists from the AFT and NEA, including national staff, state and local officers, and rank-and-file members.

The working draft outlined seven "key components of social justice unionism." The first three components give a flavor of the document, arguing that social justice unionism should:

1. Defend the rights of its members while fighting for the rights and needs of the broader community and students.

2. Recognize that the parents and neighbors of our students are key allies, and build strategic alliances with parents, labor unions, and community groups.

3. Fully involve rank-and-file members in running the union and initiate widespread discussion on how education unions should respond to the crises in education and society.

I see social justice unionism as moving beyond a "trade-union" or "professional" perspective to a "class-conscious" perspective. This class-consciousness recognizes that teachers' long-term interests are closer to those of poor and working people whose children are in our public schools, than to the corporate leaders and politicians who run our society. It views parents and community as essential partners in reform, with a stress in urban areas on developing ties with communities of color. It is committed to a bottom-up, grassroots mobilization — of teachers, parents, community, and rank-and-file union members.

Essential to social justice unionism is a recognition that schools have played a dual, contradictory role in society. On the one hand, they reinforce and reproduce class, racial, and gender divisions and inequality. On the other hand, they provide an opportunity to break down those divisions and inequalities. For all their faults, public schools are one of the most local, democratically controlled institutions in society. They are a constant battleground of competing visions and priorities.

A social justice perspective struggles against those practices that mirror and replicate society's inequalities — practices such as tracking, narrowly defined standards, infatuation with standardized testing, and admissions requirements for public schools. Further, a social justice perspective mobilizes teachers and parents to overturn such inequitable policies. How a union positions itself in such educational debates will demonstrate whether the union is serious about educating all children or whether it is merely paying lip service to such a goal.

A social justice unionism approach, for example, would caution against knee-jerk reactions by teachers and their unions to complicated matters such as student discipline, and would call for safeguards against racial or class biases in any policy. A social justice approach would also challenge long-established practices of teachers that condone and perpetuate tracking, and demand feasible alternatives. It would be wary of some union leaders' tendencies to comfortably co-exist with corporate or conservative approaches to standards and high-stakes testing.

Teacher Accountability

How might the differences in these three approaches play out on a particular issue? Looking at teacher accountability provides some clues.

Those advocating a more professional approach have focused on teacher accountability as a primary concern. Authors Kerchner and Koppich note that, traditionally, teacher unions have tended towards an industrial union model of accountability. This model sees accountability as the responsibility of principals and supervisors, not teachers. (It is sometimes referred to as an "external" accountability system, because it comes from outside of the teaching corps.)

Clearly, unions have the legal and ethical responsibility to protect the due process rights of all teachers, even incompetent teachers. In practice, however, this traditional, industrial approach to accountability has meant that the unions have taken a hands-off approach to doing anything at all about ensuring a qualified teaching corps. The industrial union response generally has been, "That's management's problem." The truth of the matter, however, is that most principals find it uncomfortable to confront bad teaching practices and often don't follow established procedures for getting rid of incompetent teachers. Most traditional teacher accountability systems dance around the hard issues of teacher quality and instead focus on the technicalities of the dismissal process.

Those advocating professional unionism argue that teacher unions must look beyond the self-interest of individual teachers and consider the broader needs of schools and children. They respect and honor the rights to due process, but also promote "internal" teacher- and union-based controls on quality. Some of the mechanisms they have used include peer mentoring, peer evaluation, and career ladders. (See articles on these innovations in the "Promising Practices" section, beginning on page 31). One of the clear advantages of peer review is that moves the dialog away

JEAN-CLAUDE LEJEUNE

from procedural technicalities of the dismissal process, and instead focuses on the substance of teaching and how to improve that teaching.

While a professional approach stresses "internal" accountability over the "external" control of a principal, a social justice approach might add additional components. It would suggest that parents and community have input in teacher evaluation.

The Rochester Teachers Association, for example, negotiated a provision in their contract to encourage parent input in teacher evaluation. The provision involves soliciting parent input in teacher/home communication and homework matters. It is an important step in recognizing that parents should be more than just homework helpers and pizza fund-raisers. (A related issue that unions are increasingly dealing with is overall parent participation in schools, in particular setting up structures so parent voices are truly listened to and respected. Such questions have been particularly complicated because of the racial and class contradictions of schools, and in some districts because of organizing by religious right forces against progressive programs and teachers.)

A social justice perspective also holds that unions should promote accountability and equity on a district-wide level. For example, the Cincinnati Federation of Teachers conducted a survey to determine which high schools were offering calculus and advanced language courses. The survey found that predominantly lower-income neighborhood schools were not offering these classes while specialty schools and the college-prep high school were. The union's subsequent organizing around the issue caused a major policy shift in the Cincinnati Public Schools, which instituted a special allocation to schools to ensure the availability of advanced classes at all schools.

The Issue of Race

How to deal with racism and race relations is a daunting problem for any institution in this country. It is particularly difficult for schools and teachers.

Teacher-union relations with communities of color have been particularly affected by an approach that prioritizes the interests and rights of teachers above the concerns of students and community.

The most prominent example in recent decades was the 1968 Ocean Hill-Brownsville strike in New York City. The conflict centered on the extent to which local communities (in this case, mainly African-American communities) could control their schools, particularly with respect to staffing. The union was opposed to community control, arguing parents should not make staffing decisions. The union won the battle, but at a daunting price. To this day, this strike is often cited as an example of the insensitivity of white-dominated unions to the community's legitimate concerns over the education of its children.

The controversy over staffing often is connected to issues of seniority. In Boston, for example, the teachers union went to court in the early 1980s to overturn programs that attempted to sustain the number of teachers of color, via a system of "super-seniority" in lay-offs. Such a "super-seniority" approach was designed to replace the traditional system of "last hired, first fired," because teachers of color tended to have less seniority.

More recently, in Milwaukee, the union has yet to fully recover from the repercussions of its decisions in the early 1990s regarding staffing at two innovative African-American immersion schools. The schools were specifically set up to deal with the high academic failure rates among African Americans, especially males. Because of the unique nature of the schools, there was a request that one-third of the schools' teachers be

African American. The union opposed the request because it violated contract provisions that set a maximum percentage, ranging from 23 to 28 percent, of African-American staff at district schools. Many in the African-American community still cite the controversy as an example of why the union cannot be trusted to care about the education of African-American children — even though in recent years an African-American woman has been elected union president and the union has shown increasing flexibility. For example, in 1999 the Milwaukee union negotiated a contract provision which allows school-based committees to side-step seniority to hire staff based on their compatibility with the school's mission and needs (see contract-language excerpt, page 64).

Professional unionism — as a whole — tends to downplay issues of race. When asked, advocates will often note the importance of race. But documents, written discussions, and conference topics, generally fail to highlight the centrality of race. For example, in Chase's speech announcing the NEA's new unionism, the issue of race is not even mentioned once. Likewise, documents of the Teacher Union Reform Network rarely talk about race directly.

In contrast, a social justice union approach would directly take on issues of race. The British Columbia Teacher's Federation, for instance, runs an education program which deals with race on personal, political, and pedagogical levels. Through a combination of workshops, training sessions, policy statements, and youth organizing, the provincial union has encouraged teachers to discuss and deal with race issues. (See article, p. 52.) Another example, albeit on a smaller scale, is the Cleveland Teachers Union's development and distribution of a teaching guide on African-centered/multiculturalism curriculum in 1995.

A key priority of social justice unionism is building coalitions and alliances with parent and community advocacy groups that speak to both school reform and ensuring equity in society as a whole. There are, unfortunately, not a plethora of examples showing such alliances. But some unions have taken noteworthy and positive steps to reach out to their logical allies. For example, the California Teachers Association and the Washington Education Association worked against statewide referenda prohibiting affirmative action. On a local level, some union locals have aggressively supported programs to recruit teachers of color, building ties with community groups in the process.

Conclusion

Historically, teacher unions have operated on the premise that their overarching responsibility is to protect their members. I would argue, however, that in the long run, unions will be able to do so only if they adopt a social justice model.

Unions are under ferocious attack and will not survive unless they are seen as advocates of school reform. Of necessity they must adopt more responsibility for the teaching profession and the academic achievement of students. Further, only by building alliances with community and parents will unions be able to withstand the conservative onslaught.

But even the best-run school district in the world cannot, over time, compensate for all the inequalities in our society — which is why a commitment to social justice must go beyond education and reach into all aspects of society. If teachers want true equal educational opportunity for their students, they must work for equal opportunity throughout society, not just in education but in health care, employment, and housing.

Social justice unionism also makes sense on a more individual level. Teachers, as all workers, want to go home at night and know they have been successful during the day. When their students live in poverty and without health care, when their students are without hope because they see unemployment everywhere in their community — then the teachers' job is all the more difficult.

In the past, other unions have faced difficult challenges and set ambitious goals. Today, teacher unions face a similar challenge. We must demand and build a democratic teacher union movement that recognizes its interests are bound up with the interests of the children and communities we serve. Only then will we be able to gather sufficient forces to ensure that public education gets the resources that schools deserve and that children need. **TTU**

BOB PETERSON TEACHES 5TH GRADE IN THE MILWAUKEE PUBLIC SCHOOLS AND IS AN EDITOR OF RETHINKING SCHOOLS. HE'S BEEN A TEACHER UNION ACTIVIST FOR NEARLY TWO DECADES.

Resources

Kerchner, C. and Julia Koppich. *A Union of Professionals: Labor Relations and Educational Reform* (New York: Teachers College Press, 1993).

Murphy, Marjorie. *Blackboard Unions, the AFT and the NEA 1900 - 1980* (Ithaca, NY: Cornell University Press, 1990).

A Hard Lesson from History

BY BOB PETERSON

A FRIEND WHO WORKS FOR A TEACHERS UNION recounted a discussion in which an anti-union teacher asked my friend why she supported unions. Her reply was simple. She said that without unions, particularly the one her dad had been in, she would have grown up in poverty.

For many that's reason enough to support unions. It's an issue of survival and has been for 150 years, since the birth of the labor movement in the United States. But the labor movement's track record of promoting the general welfare of working people is uneven, as some people, particularly people of color and women, have been excluded or discriminated against by certain unions.

I saw this first hand when I worked on the Milwaukee docks in the early 1970s. I witnessed the International Longshoreman Association's resistance to allowing women into the union. The ILA was continuing a long, nefarious tradition of some sections of organized labor. One of the first strikes in Milwaukee, for example, was in 1863 by typesetters at the *Milwaukee Sentinel* who struck to protest the hiring of women.

In these cases, the unions weren't just defending workers from greedy bosses but were also "defending" unionized workers from other workers. Historian Robert Allen, in his book, *Reluctant Reformers: Racism and Social Reform Movements in the United States* (New York: Anchor Books, 1975), documents how in many unions throughout much of the 19th and 20th century, white workers attempted to keep workers of color out of many jobs. As late as 1931, Allen notes, 14 national unions prohibited African Americans from membership.

This has been a historical weakness of unionism in the United States — fighting to improve conditions for certain poor and working people while undercutting the interests of other poor and working people. In other words, the dilemma of defending the interests of a sector of working people instead of the interests of all. Or put more generally, the issue of developing a social pact for some versus social justice for all. Often this problem is racialized.

When unions have overcome this weakness and united workers regardless of race or gender — as did the Congress of Industrial Organization during the 1930s — they became powerful social forces. Many workers in these unions had both an understanding of themselves as workers and a sense of social justice.

Teacher unions have faced similar issues. In the early 1960s, for example, there were still 11 segregated

National Education Association (NEA) state associations; as late as 1974 the NEA still had a segregated Louisiana Association. (In the past quarter century, the NEA has changed dramatically, as exemplified in its affirmative-action staff hiring policies and in guaranteeing significant minority representation at its national conventions.)

But this historic dilemma for the labor movement — balancing the survival of its members with broader issues of justice for working people as a whole — still persists. For teacher unions, the dilemma rests no longer in exclusion policies or segregated locals, but in a more complex way: how teacher unions can defend their members' rights while advocating for the broader community, in particular the needs of students. Resolving this historic dilemma is particularly important given the crescendo of attacks on public schools and teacher unions.

Teachers need to recognize that their self-interests can no longer be defined using solely "narrow trade-union" or even "professional" terms. Our interests and our future require teacher unions to adopt a social justice perspective that places the education and welfare of our students in school and in society at the top of our agenda.

My friend who works for a teachers union and who argued about the value of unions did not only talk about her father's union. She talked of how early teacher-union activists were mainly women, many of whom were involved in the suffragist movement. She explained the broader labor movement's influence on social policy legislation such as the minimum wage, unemployment compensation, and Social Security. She noted how the United Auto Workers were major backers of Dr. Martin Luther King, Jr. and the civil rights movement.

It is in the tradition of that sector of the labor movement — the one that promotes social justice for all — that we should situate our teacher unions. **TTU**

Networking for Union Reform: The Story of TURN

BY BARBARA MINER

IN MARCH 1995, ADAM URBANSKI OF THE ROCHESTER Teachers Association wrote an essay in *Education Week* laying out a vision for teachers and teacher unions. He wrote of the union as an agent of reform, of teaching as a genuine profession, and of the responsibility of both teachers and unions to ensure that all children are learning. At the time, such ideas were heresy among some teacher unionists — after all, this was a full two years before National Education Association President Bob Chase gave his controversial "new unionism" speech.

In his *Education Week* essay, Urbanski wrote, "Any vision is only a pipe dream unless created twice: first in the mind and then in the real world." First was the task of changing minds. As a start, in 1996 Urbanski, along with the late Helen Bernstein of Los Angeles and other forward-thinking unionists, founded the Teacher Union Reform Network. Composed of 21 local union presidents from both the NEA and AFT, TURN is dedicated to moving beyond the adversarial, industrial, bread-and-butter approach that dominates teacher union politics. Instead, TURN seeks to transform unions into champions of school reform, teacher professionalism, and student achievement.

Now, almost five years after the *Education Week* essay, TURN is about to move into the uncharted terrain of changing the real world. At its meeting in the Spring of 1999, TURN began building "local action plans" for each of its member locals, with a special emphasis on increased student achievement.

"We are now in a pivotal stage," Urbanski says of TURN. "This will be our transition from rhetoric to action. Our conversations have been inordinately stimulating and rewarding. But we recognize the need to go beyond conversation."

It's a tall order, and TURN has any number of minefields it must navigate. Whether it will succeed is uncertain. But one thing is clear: some of the most creative and ambitious thinking about the transformation of teacher unions is taking place among the leaders and members of TURN.

TURN's Orientation

TURN describes itself as "a union-led effort to restructure the nation's teachers' unions to promote reforms that will ultimately lead to better learning and higher achievement for America's children." Beneath the deceptively placid rhetoric is a fundamental mind

JEAN-CLAUDE LEJEUNE

shift.

Traditionally, teacher unions have focused on protecting the rights of their members — such as fighting for better pay or making sure principals did not arbitrarily fire or discipline teachers. Ensuring that all students were learning was seen for the most part as the responsibility of management (school boards, superintendents, central office administrators, and principals.) Likewise, professional development was seen as management's job. Finally, under the traditional union view, reform was something that happened *to* teachers, not something that unions initiated.

When urban schools and teacher unions came under increasing criticism in the 1980s and 1990s, some union locals reacted by adopting a "circle the wagons" mentality. They advocated that the teacher unions maintain their industrial, adversarial focus — only do it better, so to speak, and flex more muscle. TURN members had a different idea. They believed that teacher unions needed to be restructured so that they promoted, not resisted, reforms.

Some of TURN's core concepts, articulated from the very beginning:

• The adversarial labor/management culture must be replaced with collaborative approaches involving all the stakeholders in public education.

• Unions are essential partners in transforming public education and must become agents of reform.

• Teachers are professionals, and the union has a responsibility to help ensure a high quality of professionalism among all members.

• The ultimate goal must be improved student learning.

TURN's 21 locals are mostly from urban areas. They range in size from New York City's UFT, with over one million students, to the local in Westerly, RI, with 3,430 students. Urbanski is currently TURN Director. Funding has been provided by the PEW Charitable Trusts and, more recently, the John D. and Catherine T. MacArthur Foundation. The national NEA and AFT have also provided funding and support.

From its inception, TURN has developed a collaborative approach toward universities and university-based research, in particular with the UCLA Graduate School of Education and Information Studies and groups such as the Center for Policy Research in Education at the University of Wisconsin-Madison.

To date, TURN has mainly functioned as a network and support group for progressive union leaders. The group meets three times a year to discuss practice and collectively develop ideas on how to ensure that teacher unions promote school reform and increased student achievement. It also has an ever-growing website and email network, and has recently begun experimenting with regional conferences and meetings. This will allow broader participation beyond the formal members of TURN.

There are three main "work groups" within TURN: ensuring teacher quality, rethinking teacher compensation, and the union's role in professional development. Special study has also been done on developing innovative contract language.

TURN's membership list reads like a who's who of union innovators — from Tom Mooney in Cincinnati (pioneering career ladder reforms, see page 33); to Roger Erskine in Seattle (advocating flexibility in teacher seniority, see page 58); to Louise Sundin in Minneapolis (building a bold program of professional development, see page 40); to David Sherman of the UFT, Dal Lawrence of Columbus, Ohio, and Pat Tornillo of Florida.

Since its founding, TURN has taken an ecumenical approach toward what is sometimes seen as a rivalry between the AFT and NEA. Politics, not union affiliation, is what matters.

Accomplishments, Challenges

Urbanski cites three main accomplishments of TURN.

• First, that the network has survived. Urbanski jokes that when he and Helen Bernstein first talked of the idea of a network, "We speculated it would last a half hour, or maybe two hours. This was terra incognita

TURN MISSION STATEMENT

Teacher Unions must provide leadership for the collective voice of their members. Teacher Unions have a responsibility to students, their families, and to the broader society. Teacher Unions are committed to public education as a vital element of our democracy. What unites these responsibilities is our commitment to help all children learn.

We affirm the union's responsibility to collaborate with other stakeholders in public education and to seek consistently higher levels of student achievement by:
- Improving continuously the quality of teaching.
- Promoting in public education and in the union democratic dynamics, fairness, and due process for all.
- Seeking to expand the scope of collective bargaining to include instructional and professional issues.
- Improving on an ongoing basis the terms and conditions under which both adults and children work and learn.

1998

for all of us."

• Second, work on rethinking teacher compensation. Locals involved with TURN have moved beyond the traditional approach of basing pay on seniority and number of credits. Thus in Cincinnati, for example, the union has negotiated a contract which gives extra money to "lead teachers" who take additional responsibilities in areas such as curriculum development or peer mentoring.

• Third, involving unions in the professional development of teachers. Urbanski said that TURN, working with Brown University and other research institutions, is helping to develop models "on how the teachers union can become a principal provider, or a principal maker of connections, of the right kind of professional development of teachers."

Topping the list of current priorities is the development of the "local action plans." Two other areas up for discussion are ensuring collaboration among all the stakeholders in education, and turning around the media's negative image of teachers. Regarding stakeholders, Urbanski stressed that it is essential to get all those involved in public schools — superintendents, school boards, parents, community-based organizations, politicians, and the business community — to work together with unions and teachers to build models of reform that will work. "Even if unions become substantially more responsive to current needs, without the support of other constituencies it would be like one hand clapping," Urbanski notes.

Issues of Community

In instituting its reforms, TURN faces any number of challenges. One of the trickiest is dealing with the issues of race and class that dominate urban school realities. For example, teachers in urban areas are predominantly white while the students are predominantly of color. Will increased professionalism alone resolve that contradiction? Will parents and community be equal partners, or will an emphasis on professionalism lead to a "teacher-knows-best" mentality?

There are a host of equally important questions. Will an emphasis on student achievement devolve into an acceptance of even more testing of already over-tested students? Where is the forum within TURN for discussing the purpose of schooling? Is there sufficient emphasis on the relationship between the crisis of achievement in urban schools and the crisis of poverty in our urban communities?

While issues of community and equity do not figure prominently in TURN literature, Urbanski says such issues are ever-present in TURN discussions. "We have had some deep conversations about equity and access," Urbanski says. "And what we have concluded is that we must promote equity and excellence at the same time — that excellence without equity is not excellence, it is privilege." Urbanski underscores that TURN will evaluate itself not just by how much unions contribute to student learning, but how much they can contribute to narrowing the gap between the highest performing and the lowest performing children.

Likewise, TURN members seem to be aware of the dual-nature of the higher standards movement and that it can pave the way for increased reliance on standardized tests. "We recognize that we are dealing with complex issues," Urbanski says, "and we don't want to find cures that are worse than the disease."

It is, as Urbanski notes, terra incognita. TURN realizes it may mis-step along the way. But it is not afraid to make the journey. **TTU**

BARBARA MINER IS MANAGING EDITOR OF *RETHINKING SCHOOLS*.

TURN CAN BE CONTACTED AT TURN, C/O ROCHESTER TEACHERS ASSOCIATION, 30 N. UNION STREET, SUITE 301, ROCHESTER, NEW YORK 14607. 716-546-2681; FAX: 716-546-4123; EMAIL: URBANSKI@SERVTECH.COM. INTERNET: WWW.TURNEXCHANGE.NET.

URBANSKI'S *EDUCATION WEEK* ARTICLE, "REVOLUTION OF RISING EXPECTATIONS: A VISION OF TEACHING TEN YEARS DOWN THE ROAD" CAN BE VIEWED IN THE ARCHIVE SECTION OF THE WEBSITE OF *EDUCATION WEEK* AT WWW.EDWEEK.COM.

A New Vision of Schooling

BY THE EDITORS OF *RETHINKING SCHOOLS*

ANYONE INVOLVED IN SCHOOL REFORM DISCUSSIONS knows that there's often a surplus of rhetoric and an absence of substance. To be useful, such discussions need to be not only based on classroom realities but guided by a common set of principles and goals.

Developing mutual principles and goals does several things. It creates consensus for reform priorities. It can reveal the sometimes competing agendas hidden by vague rhetoric. It also helps to clarify the criteria by which the positive or negative impact of specific reforms might be judged.

The following are starting points for what such principles might look like for the classroom, schools, districts, and the broader community.

Principle #1: The Common School

We believe that reform must be grounded in the democratic vision of "the common school." Especially at a time when racial and class inequalities are growing in our country, school reform must be about more than producing efficient workers or Nobel scientists. It must be shaped by an understanding of the crucial role public schools play in providing the cultural, social, and material support that makes a democratic society possible. Schools are the place where children from a variety of backgrounds come together and, at least in theory, learn to talk, play, and work together. Schools are integral to preparing all children not only to be full participants in society, but also to be full participants in this country's ever-tenuous experiment in multicultural democracy. That this vision has yet to be fully realized does not mean it should be abandoned.

We are aware that many powerful people extol the virtues of marketplace approaches to our schools' problems. Left to its own bottom-line logic, the market will do for educational services in poor communities only what markets have done in areas like health care or housing: create profitable opportunities for some well-financed investors, and allow a few, more fortunate education consumers to buy their way out of troubled schools. In the process, it will also reproduce the class and racial inequalities that various customers bring to the market with them, and it will weaken society's collective commitment to all our children. For these reasons we support, and will fight for, a truly public system that is accountable, democratically run, and open to all.

Principle #2: Reform must recognize the realities of the classroom and center on the needs of children.

Too many educational reforms are designed to further the careers of politicians. Sound-bites too often replace meaningful dialogue. The lens through which we should judge any educational reform is how it improves teaching and learning in the classroom.

KATHY SLOANE

jacket teachers, and bully students. We need to promote rigorous, *classroom-based* assessments that support good instructional practices, provide clear information to students and teachers, and show parents and the community that our students are learning.

Principle #4: Teacher Professionalism and Accountability.

No reform is more important than that of improving the quality of teaching. This includes ensuring that teachers are certified and educated in the areas they teach, that teacher education institutions prepare prospective teachers for the realities of classroom life, that school staffs are part of a process to develop a common vision of teaching as a solid foundation for collaboration and accountability, that teachers have time for ongoing professional development and to collaborate with their colleagues on a regular basis, that all teachers be educated to be more culturally sensitive, that mentor programs be instituted for all new teachers, and that peer assistance and review programs be put in place.

In addition, given the small percentage of teachers of color (13%) compared to the percentage of students of color (35%) in public schools, all stakeholders need to work to increase the number of certified teachers of color.

Unions need to ensure that classroom teachers have the time to collaborate and improve their practice and have a place at the table for major educational reform discussions.

Principle #3: Reform must be based on a commitment to equity and high standards for all children.

We know how to teach children well, but unfortunately too many children have been given up as lost. We need high expectations, rigorous curriculum, adequate resources, and a culture of collaboration and mutual accountability.

Standards should be set and implemented to improve outcomes for all children, rather than to reinforce the tendency of schools to sort and label students in ways that reproduce the social inequality around us. High standards can have a positive impact on curriculum, classroom practice, and student expectations only where they are paired with improved educational programs and services. Without real improvements in the conditions of teaching and learning, higher standards driven by high-stakes, multiple-choice tests distort the curriculum, strait-

Principle #5: Adequate and equal resources for all schools and classrooms.

Money, well spent, matters. The quality of a public school should not be based on the quirks of geography. It is unjust that many urban and rural districts can only spend half as much per pupil as affluent suburban districts — especially when their needs for resources may be substantially greater. One of the most glaring contradictions of the reform movement is the gap between the rising expectations for schools and the conspicuous absence of the resources to achieve them. There needs to be more money for facilities, reducing class size, and staff development; less for testing and for unproven, politically motivated experiments like vouchers and charters.

Educators, in turn, must recognize that money is necessary but insufficient for reform.

Principle #6: Reform must involve collaboration among educators, parents, and community members.

Lasting reform must be built from the ground up. It should be based on respect and collaboration among administrators, teachers, parents, and community members. Parents, in particular, have been marginalized in school reform efforts, and must be brought into the decision-making process, both on a district-wide and school level. We should encourage guarantees for all workers to days of paid leave in order to attend parent-teacher conferences and help out at their children's schools. The United Auto Workers have negotiated such provisions in some of their contracts.

Principle #7: Create community schools as locations of neighborhood vitality and community renaissance.

In many urban neighborhoods, public schools and churches are among the few stable institutions that remain. These schools should be renovated and transformed into full-service community centers. Schools should be equipped to serve the entire community — from the youngest toddlers to adults and the elderly — in a variety of recreational, cultural, and social service ways. Such new schools could become social anchors in struggling neighborhoods — community centers open seven days a week. The possibilities are endless: quality child care, before- and after-school programs, neighborhood linkups to the World Wide Web, adult education classes, recreational and art programs, social services, and a place where the community comes together to learn, organize, and put notions of real democracy into action. Such inter-generational centers would have the added benefit of putting urban and rural schools on par with suburban schools by including modern libraries, art, music, and multi-purpose rooms.

Principle #8: Smaller class sizes.

Smaller classes make sense: when there are few children in a classroom, a teacher can better meet the needs of individual students. The STAR study in Tennessee and the SAGE program in Wisconsin have found that smaller classes are especially beneficial to children in inner-city schools. Combined with other supports for teaching and learning, smaller class sizes can significantly improve the likelihood of higher student achievement.

Principle #9: Our urban communities, not just our urban schools, are in crisis.

In the long run, the health of our schools reflects the health of the communities they serve. Joblessness, poverty, substance abuse, and sub-standard housing are undeniable factors in the problems of our urban schools. Teacher unions must work in alliance with other labor unions, community groups, churches and civic leaders to boldly address these problems. Supporting living-wage campaigns is one such example.

Principle #10: Classrooms and curriculum should be geared towards learning for life.

A good curriculum is based on a number of assumptions. These include:

• **Grounded in the lives of our students.** All good teaching begins with a respect for children, their innate curiosity, and their capacity to learn. Curriculum should be rooted in children's needs and experiences. Whether we're teaching science, mathematics, English, or social studies, ultimately the class has to be about our students' lives as well as about a particular subject. Students should probe the ways their lives connect to the broader society.

• **Critical.** The curriculum should equip students to "talk back" to the world. Students must learn to pose essential critical questions: Who makes decisions and who is left out? Who benefits and who suffers? Why is a given practice fair or unfair? What are its origins? What alternatives can we imagine? What is required to create change? Through critiques of advertising, cartoons, literature, legislative decisions, military interventions, job structures, newspapers, movies, business practices, trade policies, or school life, students should have opportunities to question social reality. Finally, student work must move outside the classroom walls, so that scholastic learning is linked to real world problems.

• **Committed to social justice.** A social justice curriculum must strive to include the lives of all those in our society, especially the marginalized and domi-nated. Explicitly multicultural and anti-racist, a social justice curriculum should engage children in a critique of the roots of inequality in curriculum, school structure, and the larger society — always asking: How are we involved? What can we do?

• **Participatory, experiential.** Traditional classrooms often leave little room for student involvement and initiative. In a "rethought" classroom, concepts need to be experienced first-hand, not just read about or heard about. Whether through projects, role plays, simulations, mock trials, or experiments, students need to be mentally, and often physically, active. Our classrooms

There is a Zulu expression: "If the future doesn't come toward you, you have to go fetch it."

also must provoke students to develop their democratic capacities: to question, to challenge, to make real decisions, to solve problems collectively.

• **Hopeful, joyful, kind, visionary.** The ways we organize classroom life should seek to make children feel significant and cared about — by the teacher and by each other. Unless students feel emotionally and physically safe, they won't share real thoughts and feelings. Discussions will be shallow and dishonest. We need to design activities where students learn to trust and care for each other. Classroom life should, to the greatest extent possible, pre-figure the kind of democratic and just society we envision and thus contribute to building that society. Together, students and teachers can create a "community of conscience."

• **Activist.** We want students to come to see themselves as truth-tellers and change-makers. If we ask children to critique the world but then fail to encourage them to act, our classrooms can degenerate into factories for cynicism. While it's not a teacher's role to direct students to particular organizations, it is a teacher's role to suggest that ideas should be acted upon and to offer students opportunities to do just that. Children can also draw inspiration from historical and contemporary efforts of people who struggled for justice. A critical curriculum should be a rainbow of resistance, reflecting the diversity of people from all cultures who acted — often at a great sacrifice — to make a difference. Students should be allowed to learn about and feel connected to this legacy of defiance.

• **Academically rigorous.** A social justice classroom equips children not only to change the world but also to maneuver in the one that exists. Far from devaluing the vital academic skills young people need, a critical and activist curriculum speaks directly to the deeply rooted alienation that currently discourages millions of students from acquiring those skills.

• **Culturally sensitive.** Critical teaching requires that we admit we don't know it all. Each class presents new challenges to learn from our students and demands that we be good researchers and good listeners. These days, the demographic reality of schooling makes it likely that white teachers will enter classrooms filled with children of color. To best teach children who are different from themselves, teachers must understand that parents are important colleagues who can help them learn who their students really are. Teachers must also call upon culturally diverse co-workers and community resources for insights into the communities they seek to serve. What can be said about racial and cultural differences between teachers and students also holds true for class differences.

There is a Zulu expression. "If the future doesn't come toward you, you have to go fetch it." We believe teachers, parents, and students are essential to building a movement to go fetch a better future: in our classrooms, in our schools, and in the larger society. There are lots of us out here. Let's make our voices heard. **TTU**

FOR A FULLER EXPLANATION OF HOW THE CURRICULAR POINTS DESCRIBED IN PRINCIPLE 10 CAN BE USED TO GUIDE TEACHING IN SCHOOLS, SEE *RETHINKING OUR CLASSROOMS: TEACHING FOR EQUITY AND JUSTICE,* AVAILABLE FROM RETHINKING SCHOOLS BY VISITING ITS WEBSITE AT WWW.RETHINKINGSCHOOLS.ORG.

KIRK ANDERSON

Promising Practices

Raising Professional Standards

BY TOM MOONEY

IN ANOTHER ERA, THE INJUNCTION TO "ACT PROFESSION-ally" was management's mantra. It meant, of course, "do what you're told, don't dissent, and never think of joining a trade union."

In the context of school reform currents in the late 1980s and '90s, professionalism took on a much different meaning. Al Shanker and at least some local leaders in both unions infused a hefty dose of professionalism into trade unionism by adopting peer review, creating differentiated roles, responsibilities, and pay (through negotiated career ladders), lobbying for higher standards to enter teaching, and supporting the National Board for Professional Teaching Standards to recognize advanced practitioners, among other measures. Under Bob Chase, NEA policy has turned decisively in the same direction, while at AFT, Sandy Feldman is even more engaged in encouraging and helping locals to take the initiative on school reform.

As a crisis of confidence in public education has grown more and more serious, raising professional standards for teachers has been a key element of our school reform strategy, along with more rigorous academic and behavior standards for students and changes in school organization and teaching methods. These reforms have enabled us to pose a credible alternative to privatization of schooling on the one hand and bureaucratic versions of reform on the other.

This new professional unionism was both inspired by and helped to inspire the more thoughtful currents in the education reform movement of the past fifteen years, exemplified by the 1986 Carnegie Report (*A Nation Prepared: Teachers for the 21st Century*), the Holmes Reports on reform of teacher preparation, and more recently, the report of the National Commission on Teaching and America's Future (*What Matters Most*).

It is also fueled by a growing body of research that points to teacher quality as the most important factor in student achievement gains. (Family income and

JEAN-CLAUDE LEJEUNE

parents' level of education remain the most reliable predictors of current status, but teacher quality powerfully influences improvement rates.)

Professionalism offers an answer to the accountability question, i.e. that professionals are accountable to their clients. Advocates of market-based reforms — vouchers, tuition tax credits, and privately operated charter schools — say letting parents choose any public or private school is the only way to hold schools accountable. Bureaucratic reformers still have faith in traditional management structures. "Let us hold those teachers accountable, abolish tenure (better yet, deunionize), free up those principals to get rid of the dead wood, fine tune that management structure ... and we'll make the system hum." Although its many iterations have been tried many times, this approach is still popular among school administrators, school board members, and some corporate leaders interested in school reform, so local union leaders deal with it every day.

In the context of union-led school reform, professionalism calls out the best impulses in our memberships, allowing us to win majority support for the necessary changes in union policies that pave the way for advancing creative and sometimes bold proposals at the bargaining table or in public policy arenas. It builds on teachers' desire for professional respect, status, and pay, but also appeals to their commitment to kids. It challenges and empowers teachers to adopt research-based best practices rather than clinging to tradition or being pushed to adopt the latest fads.

Reform-minded union leaders have adopted professionalism as a lever to move our own members in a progressive direction. It has also been a powerful tool. It has helped us make a case for reaching out to parents and participating in struggles to improve our students' lives outside of school. Teacher quality is one of the key equity or social justice issues in education. Poor and minority students are much more likely to have uncertified, out-of-field, or inexperienced teachers.

For AFT locals, participation in the broader labor movement also drives our involvement with broader social issues. It's hard not to get drawn into battles for

school funding equity, worthy wages for child-care workers, anti-sweatshop campaigns, exposing tax abatements and other corporate welfare, etc.

Yes, professionalism rests in part on the self-interest of teachers, but any good organizing strategy must appeal to self-interest as well as broader social interests and solidarity.

In my experience, professionalism (accountability to our clients) is the most powerful framework for winning teachers to the movement for meaningful education reform, which may be the key to saving public education. TTU

TOM MOONEY IS PRESIDENT OF THE CINCINNATI FEDERATION OF TEACHERS AND A VICE PRESIDENT OF THE AFT. HIS TWO CHILDREN ATTEND CINCINNATI PUBLIC SCHOOLS. THE ABOVE IS AN EDITED EXCERPT FROM A LONGER ARTICLE FIRST PUBLISHED IN THE FALL/WINTER 1998 EDITION OF *NEW LABOR FORUM*.

JEAN-CLAUDE LEJEUNE

Teachers as Leaders in Cincinnati

BY MONICA SOLOMON

AT BRAMBLE DEVELOPMENTAL ACADEMY, A SMALL neighborhood elementary school on the east side of Cincinnati, Lead Teacher Rosaland Robinson is scurrying around her sixth grade classroom with enthusiasm and energy, teaching today's mathematics lesson. "Aaron, please read the directions aloud.... Who's ready to go to the board and solve the equation?"

Robinson, a 26-year veteran, never sits down. She walks between tables, talking, listening, outwardly praising students while gently reminding them to keep the noise level down. Silence prevails. While students work at the board, Robinson confers with a Xavier University education major, who has been assigned to observe her classroom. When her students leave her classroom, Robinson's day is far from over. She supervises the school's extended day program, facilitates a grueling budgeting session with colleagues as chair of the Instructional Leader Team, and makes telephone calls to certain parents. She estimates she'll be home by 7:00 p.m.

A little north of town at a magnet middle school called Shroder Paideia, Lead Teacher Barb Scholtz arrives at 7:00 a.m. Scholtz explained that she "serves the teachers and students to improve student achievement" in a variety of ways. She oversees four of nine graduate student interns from a teacher preparation program at the University of Cincinnati. She serves as a team leader and coach for a seventh-eighth grade team. She also coordinates curriculum and professional development, recruits new students, holds disciplinary conferences with students and parents, and is a member of the local school decision-making committee and the Instructional Leadership Team. Come 5:00 p.m., Scholtz is not ready to leave school until she's tutored two former students who are struggling to pass the Ohio Ninth Grade Proficiency Test.

It's a typical 12-hour day for Robinson and Scholtz, doing what their peers say they do best — teach,

model, listen, lead. They have earned "lead teacher" status and are part of Cincinnati Public Schools' Career in Teaching program, a joint project of the district and the Cincinnati Federation of Teachers (CFT). Negotiated as part of the teacher contract in 1989, the Career in Teaching program is designed to create a professional leadership corps within the active teaching profession and to provide incentives to keep

RICK REINHARD

CAREER IN TEACHING: HOW IT WORKS IN CINCINNATI

Teachers progress through Intern, Resident, Career Teacher, and Lead Teacher levels, with financial rewards at each step, based on a combination of assessment, advanced education, and experience.

Interns, all teachers new to the Cincinnati Public Schools, are assisted and evaluated by consulting teachers. They must pass the internship with a satisfactory rating within two years, at the latest.

Then, teachers continue to develop as Residents and receive their first salary increase. Advancing to Career Level (and tenure) requires a teacher to pass an evaluation by the principal, complete 30 graduate semester hours related to his or her teaching field, and teach for at least three years with

(cont. on next page)

excellent teachers in the classroom.

"Lead teachers are the change agents within the school," said CFT Professional Issues Representative Denise Hewitt. "They are the first line in terms of change, curriculum, mentoring, providing resources, and initiating professional development. They are the ones others — students and colleagues — look up to." Hewitt said that with the district's current pace of reform, including local school decision-making, team-based schools, smaller central office, and decentralized student-based budgeting, the role of the lead teacher is even more paramount to the overall improvement of a school.

Higher Standards for Teachers

For years, the only way teachers in the Cincinnati Public Schools could advance their careers was to move to administration, either by becoming a principal or assistant principal or by going to central office. By the late 1980s, the district and the teachers union recognized the need to keep talented teachers in classrooms and schools and allow teachers to play leadership roles within their profession. The timing was right; shortly after launching the Career in Teaching program in 1990, Cincinnati Public Schools' drastically cut central administration by 50%, with the goal of pushing more resources and decision-making to local schools.

CFT President Tom Mooney said there was a mutual interest to change the culture of the teaching profession, reduce teacher attrition, and keep the best teachers in school by rewarding them. "Our goal was to cultivate a cadre of instructional leaders within the ranks of practitioners," Mooney said.

Teachers in the Career in Teaching program progress through Intern, Resident, Career Teacher, and Lead Teacher levels, with increased financial rewards at each step, based on a combination of assessment, advanced education, and experience. Only those teachers with at least six years in teaching — the last three in the district — can apply for lead teacher status. An extensive application is reviewed by the Career in Teaching Panel, made up of three administrators and three teachers. If the application meets all criteria,

the teacher is observed by a skilled veteran teacher called Trained Teacher Observer (TTO), who also interviews the applicant's principal and several teaching colleagues. Highly proficient teachers with demonstrated leadership ability are then recommended by the TTOs for lead teacher status.

Of the 3,500 teachers in Cincinnati Public Schools, currently 417 teachers have lead teacher credentials; 277 are actually serving in lead teacher positions. Only credentialed lead teachers can apply for professional leadership roles created by an agreement between the school district and CFT. Lead teachers serve in a variety of roles including interdisciplinary team leaders, subject area leaders, primary (K-3) and intermediate (4-6) level leaders, curriculum development specialists, instructors in professional development, consulting teachers, curriculum council chairs and facilitators of new or special programs. Lead teachers also serve as consulting teachers as part of the district's Peer Assistance and Evaluation Program.

A Team Approach to Tough Decisions

The career ladder program gives teachers a much greater voice in setting direction for Cincinnati Public Schools. Nowhere are their voices heard more than in local schools, in particular, the district's Team-based Schools. A central focus of Cincinnati Public Schools' five-year plan, Team-based Schools have few restrictions in terms of staffing models and budget allocation. Teams of three to five teachers stay with and take responsibility for a common group of students for an entire instructional level.

Both Robinson and Scholtz work in Team-based Schools where the role of the lead teacher takes on even greater meaning. For them, accountability and ownership are part of their daily routine, especially as chairs of their schools' Instructional Leadership Team (ILT). The ILT — consisting of the principal, lead teachers, union building representative, parent representative, and non-teaching employee — develops, reviews, and evaluates programs, practices, and procedures for effective operation of the school and the continued improvement of instruction.

As ILT chairpersons, Robinson and Scholtz are charged with building consensus around difficult issues. For example, this year both schools are faced with cuts as part of the district's new student-based budgeting model.

"A $35,000 cut is a blow to our school," Robinson sighed. "We're a small school and 85 percent of our budget is staff; that does not leave us much in reserve." Facing one of her biggest challenges to date, she is determined to build consensus among her colleagues to make tough monetary decisions — such as eliminating a position — and do what's best for kids. "We'll have to work hard to reach and stand by our decisions, cope with our decisions, and help other to do the same," she said.

Kathleen Ware, Cincinnati Public Schools District Associate Superintendent of Schools, said that there is a great deal of power in making decisions on resource allocation. And she recognizes the difficulty team leaders have in this area, "but teachers must have the authority to determine how to use the resources to get the kids to meet the standards." Shroder Paideia Principal Ray Spicher said lead teachers play a major role in getting and sustaining academic results. "The bottom line — having teachers in leadership roles — improves student learning and causes each teacher in the team to be accountable for academic achievement and discipline," he said.

Working As Peers

Spicher also acknowledges that the career ladder program changes the role of the principal in a school. "As principals, we have to make the paradigm shift from sole decision-making to empowering others to make decisions for the betterment of the school," he said. "Sure I struggle with having that tight control, but letting go of that autocratic attitude provides a more professional atmosphere where teachers and principals see each other as valuable resources to talk and plan about teaching and learning," Spicher said.

For Lead Teacher Scholtz, being a lead teacher is an integral part in the peer development process. She acknowledges having

learned a great deal over the years. "You have to learn to listen, to delegate, to develop an aura of camaraderie that keeps everyone moving toward the continuous improvement of a school," said Scholtz. "Sometimes it is hard."

Peers listen to each other, acknowledged Christine Robertson, principal of Bramble Developmental Academy. "Teachers are often more responsive to each other than to an administrator," she said. "Lead teachers like Rosaland (Robinson) plan, communicate, help other teachers, and serve as role models in the school." That is the purpose of the team structure in the Team-based Schools, according to Associate Superintendent Ware, to foster more professional dialogue and discussion. "The weaker members of the team would learn from the stronger ones," Ware said.

Challenges Ahead

Most importantly, the Career in Teaching program is designed to be flexible to meet the needs of the school district. One of the challenges is to encourage lead teachers to transfer to more challenging schools in need, in order to facilitate the changes needed to benefit students. According to Murray Grace, Career in Teaching Program Facilitator, not all schools have lead teachers, and the challenge is "to look at every policy and procedure to get good teachers to move where there is the most need."

"Teachers are reluctant to go to a dysfunctional school, but being part of a new leadership team to turn around a school might encourage teachers to move," said CFT President Mooney. He noted the district's new School Assistance and Redesign Plan, a plan developed jointly by teacher representatives and administrators to turn around low-achieving schools. The plan recognizes high-achieving schools and schools that are improving, subjects schools with low achievement and stagnant improvement goals to program changes, and closes a handful of schools with the lowest achievement and no improvement. The School Redesign category — which closes a school, then reopens it with a newly selected team of

(cont. from prev. page)

satisfactory or better performance.

Teachers can remain at the Career Level indefinitely, but those with at least six years in teaching, the last three in the district, can apply for Lead Teacher status. An extensive application is reviewed by the Career in Teaching Panel, made up of three administrators and three teachers.

If the application meets all criteria, the teacher is observed by a skilled, veteran teacher called a Trained Teacher Observer (TTO), who also interviews the applicant's principal and several teaching colleagues. Highly proficient teachers with demonstrated leadership ability are recommended by TTOs for lead teacher status. Only credentialed lead teachers can apply for professional leadership roles created by an agreement between the CFT and school district.

a principal, teachers, and other staff — is one way to encourage lead teachers to move to low-performing schools.

Union and district leaders face a challenge not uncommon to most large-city districts — finding ways to provide professional assistance to "teachers in the middle," as CFT's Hewitt describes it. Cincinnati's nationally-recognized Peer Assistance and Evaluation Program assists teachers who are new to the district and assists tenured teachers who exhibit serious teaching deficiencies. But according to Hewitt, the teachers in the middle, who make up the vast majority of the district's 3,500 teachers, are often the teachers who can benefit the most from mentoring, coaching, and guidance from lead teachers. "What do we do with the mediocre teacher who goes into their classroom day after day, closes the door, performs well on their annual observation by the principal, but does little to affect the achievement of the students in her class?"

Hewitt said the union and the district need to work together to ensure that lead teachers are working directly with the principals to improve learning, especially in the content areas. CFT President Mooney agrees, "Our goal is to get more lead teachers observing, coaching, mentoring other teachers."

> *"Teachers are often more responsive to each other than to an administrator," says principal Robertson. "Lead teachers plan, communicate, help other teachers, and serve as role models in the school."*

In Cincinnati Public Schools, teacher evaluation is a shared responsibility of the teaching profession and the administration. The Peer Assistance and Evaluation Program has shown positive results. A recently-formed joint union-district Teacher Evaluation Committee is developing a new model to emphasize self-assessment, portfolio development, and peer coaching, to be piloted in fall 1999.

Another way to strengthen the professionalization of teaching is to offer more intensive professional development to lead teachers in coaching and mentoring. "Through professional development," said facilitator Grace, "we strive to develop a sense of collegiality among lead teachers and instill in them that they are the ones who must improve instruction for others."

In Cincinnati, Ohio, teachers are demonstrating leadership by helping others become better teachers. Back at Shroder Paideia, Lead Teacher Mary Wertheimer is reviewing intern Gary Collins' weekly lesson plan. "In what areas will students need help on the business letters?" Wertheimer asked.

Collins had yet to anticipate that part of the lesson. So Wertheimer jumped in. "They tend to switch the addresses around, the format and indentations will be a bit off, watch for capitalization in the headings, but most importantly get them to think about purpose."

Diligently recording his mentor's expertise, Collins sighed with relief. "Only a veteran teacher could know such things." TTU

KATHY SLOANE

MONICA SOLOMON IS AN EDUCATIONAL CONSULTANT SPECIALIZING IN STRATEGIC COMMUNICATIONS PLANNING. SHE RECENTLY SERVED AS DIRECTOR OF PUBLIC AFFAIRS FOR CINCINNATI PUBLIC SCHOOLS IN CINCINNATI, OHIO.

FOR MORE INFORMATION ABOUT THE PROGRAMS MENTIONED ABOVE, CONTACT: CINCINNATI FEDERATION OF TEACHERS, 1216 E. MCMILLAN STREET, ROOM 201, CINCINNATI, OHIO 45206; 513-961-2272; FAX: 513-961-0629.

A Lead Teacher Speaks Out

AN INTERVIEW WITH DIANA PORTER

Why is the team-based lead teacher program an improvement?

Before we started implementing the team-based model, our lead teachers acted more as program facilitators and worked with far too many teachers. They did things like help teachers wade through the first few years of a new textbook or adjust to a new curriculum adopted by central office. Under this previous model, their work wasn't that connected to the day-to-day life of the teachers in the classroom. The impact on student achievement was minimal.

The new team approach is much better. Under this team-based structure, the lead teachers work with maybe four other teachers and share responsibility for the success of the students. They're right in there in the middle of it. As a result, the lead teachers have to focus on improving instruction and even sometimes the interaction between the students and teachers in the classroom. In my school, we have 15 teams, which means 15 team leaders. The lead teachers don't get time off from their other teaching responsibilities, but they get a $5,000 annual stipend to compensate for all the extra responsibilities and lost preparation periods. That's a real incentive.

What role did the union play in this reform?

The career ladder program in Toledo, Ohio — the first in the state — inspired the Cincinnati Federation of Teachers to negotiate a way for teachers to have more responsibility and not leave teaching. The union pushed the idea and a joint management/union committee was formed. The union's contract-negotiating committee worked out the details. At first, principals came out kicking and screaming against the idea. However, once they saw teachers giving good leadership, the program became much more acceptable to them. They

realized that the team leaders could be important allies in efforts to improve instruction. The principals know they don't have enough time or energy to provide instructional leadership. And many of them don't have the preparation or training to give specific feedback that can improve instruction.

On the district level, meanwhile, the team teachers are providing leadership in curriculum councils and in the peer mentoring and review program.

Teachers like the program because they are able to influence reform in the district. The union has basically made it possible to advance to a new career level without having to leave teaching. It's a great reform. **TTU**

— interview by Bob Peterson

DIANA PORTER TEACHES AT THE HIGH SCHOOL FOR THE TEACHING PROFESSIONS IN CINCINNATI AND HAS BEEN ACTIVE IN THE CINCINNATI FEDERATION OF TEACHERS FOR OVER 20 YEARS.

RICK REINHARD

Unions Can Create a Sense of Hope

BY MICHAEL CHARNEY

IF TEACHER UNIONS WANT TO DEFEAT THE ORGANIZED attack on public education, we must take an active role in ensuring that schools successfully teach all children, especially poor children in urban areas.

We can't just say "vouchers are wrong." Until we have schools all parents want to send their kids to, we are going to have the threat of vouchers. Unions can't only flex our labor/political muscle. We must take on the fundamental problems of our schools.

Teacher unions are perhaps the only institutional force that has the capacity to successfully push the broad social agenda necessary to overcome these fundamental problems. Teacher unions are uniquely positioned: we are one of the largest interracial organizations in urban areas, we are connected to important constituencies of parents and the labor movement, and we have financial resources and the legal power of collective bargaining.

Moreover, unions can take advantage of the grow-ing rhetorical commitment to high standards and new state laws requiring all students to read at grade level by third or fourth grade. When states add promotion sanctions to these laws, the results will sharply reflect the class and race inequities within society. This provides an opportunity for a teachers union to mobilize its membership and the community to demand what works to achieve early literacy: a high-quality teacher working in a small class of fifteen students with organized community support and parent involvement. Such a focus on the common-ground strategy of guaranteeing equity of results in early literacy can position teacher unions as the leader of hope for children and communities.

Educators know what it will take to overcome such inequity and to improve the opportunities for the children we teach. We just have to develop the political will to do it.

What might this mean in practice? Here are three possibilities.

In many cities, superintendents or state officials are "reconstituting" failing schools. Rather than merely labeling reconstitution as an attack on teachers' rights, unions might want to take the lead on redesigning low-performing schools. We need to shape programs that will protect members and make sure they are treated fairly. But we also need to go into those schools and insist upon research-based programs that will help improve student achievement. We should motivate our members to implement such programs, even if it means changing our teaching methods. And we should demand the resources so that the children

IT TAKES A VILLAGE TO ABANDON A CHILD

Mike Ludovich

can succeed.

A second, related issue: staffing at schools where students are having the most difficulty. Teacher unions shouldn't just blindly support traditional seniority programs. Instead, we should take the lead in attracting the most motivated, most focused, and most coherent group of teachers to the schools where kids are having the most difficulties. Contractual procedures and financial incentives can be set up to get such people into the schools — and not wait until the administration, or some politician, decides to "get tough" and lower the boom on low-performing schools. At the same time, unions should steer to other schools those teachers who are not willing to make the extra effort necessary to work in low-performing schools, and make sure their rights are respected.

A third issue: bad teachers. Again, the union can't afford to stick with past practice and uncritically defend poor teachers. We have a responsibility to protect the rights of all teachers, even lousy teachers. But, if necessary, we have to say to our members: "If you are not going to provide your students the same quality instruction you'd expect for your own child, then maybe it's time to rethink whether you really want to continue teaching."

Above all, the unions have to recreate a sense of hope in our urban schools. And the best way we can do this is to take the lead in ensuring teacher quality. We need to spotlight examples of effective teaching. We need to build networks so all teachers are involved in peer review and support. We need to take collective responsibility at the building level for student achievement — and I'm not just talking about test scores, but also about what happens day in and day out in the classroom next to you. Teachers know, sometimes better than parents

or politicians, the true stories of our schools.

Hope is essential not just for our students and our communities, but for all of us who teach. If the kids we work so hard to teach do not succeed, we are going to hate our jobs. Most of us went into teaching because we want to see kids learn. Our job satisfaction is pretty low when that doesn't happen. In fact, teachers have a common interest with parents to ensure that the conditions for our students will allow them to succeed.

There is some legitimacy to the dissatisfaction with urban public education. We have to demand the resources and changes in society to make schools truly work. But we also have to hold a mirror up to ourselves and say, "What can we do differently?"

Some argue that this approach will decrease the union's ability to protect its members. But that view is based on a narrow view of protection.

The union will succeed only if our students succeed. The community needs to hear that message and see it put into practice. **TTU**

MICHAEL CHARNEY HAS BEEN A MEMBER OF THE EXECUTIVE BOARD OF THE CLEVELAND TEACHER UNION (CTU) FOR OVER A DECADE AS THE MIDDLE SCHOOL REPRESENTATIVE, AND IS A CO-EDITOR OF *TRANSFORMING TEACHER UNIONS*.

Professionalism in Minneapolis: A New View

BY KRIS BERGGREN

THE MINNEAPOLIS FEDERATION OF TEACHERS (MFT) is birthing a new vision of professionalism, from the womb of theory into the world of practice. The union has labored for over a decade to institutionalize a professional development process that aims to improve teacher quality and, thereby, student learning — and even to dramatically change the beleaguered culture that typically pervades K-12 education.

The progressive collaboration between the union and the Minneapolis Public Schools has forged a contract that since 1997 has prescribed an unusual

professional development structure. The Minneapolis plan is based on a system of peer review and ongoing assessment directly related to teachers' self-determined goals — and is backed by a $2 million-plus budget, or 2.5 percent of the entire district budget. Its success hinges on empowering more than 4,000 teachers at 104 sites to accept a high level of responsibility for their own professional growth within the context of accessible support systems. It virtually guarantees a return on investment for those who spend time and energy on the plan — and a polite escort out the door

KATHY SLOANE

for those who do not.

"The Professional Development Process (PDP) is the process of assessment in every Minneapolis school," said MFT business agent Audrey McRoy. "It puts the responsibility on the teacher to understand, 'There are things I can do to affect how our kids do.' It's important for a teacher to internalize that change in strategy and behavior."

The Minneapolis plan combats the tired tradition of teacher isolationism and subjective, often perfunctory, evaluation by a single administrator. It replaces these with peer review by the individual teacher's self-selected team, collegial support and feedback, coaching, and other strategies. The goal is to encourage self-awareness; enhanced communication with students, peers, administrators and parents; and a commitment to active learning — all designed to raise the standard of teacher quality and, consequently, student growth.

In fact, while political debate rages on the effects of class size and academic standards on student outcomes, recent research by Linda Darling Hammond and the National Commission on Teaching for America's Future indicates that teacher quality—far more than class size—is a better predictor of improved student achievement.

A Harbinger for Education Reform?

Districts elsewhere are taking note. Mark Simon, president of the Montgomery County (Maryland) Education Association and former NEA board member, visited Minneapolis last year and left with a vision.

"We were impressed for two reasons. First, they seemed to have student achievement, quality teaching, and equity concerns at the center of what drove both the union and school system," said Simon. "Secondly, the relationships between the union, district, and administrators are collaborative. I think so many school systems across the country are engaged in *sub rosa* battles where the administration is trying to put one over on the union or vice versa. Minneapolis seems to have gotten over it."

"We're designing a peer review system to pilot next September," he said. "We have a preamble to our new contract, with the core concept of 'continuous improvement,' and that language came right from the Minneapolis contract."

Labor and Management Pledge to Trust

In 1984, then-superintendent Richard Green and Louise Sundin, newly elected president of the Minneapolis Teachers' Union, appointed a task force on professionalism in teaching, with a hope of improving

relationships between the union, the school board, and the superintendent's office, .

"We pledged to start trying to trust each other," said Sundin. In 1987, they appointed an advisory committee composed of labor and management representatives, parents, students, human resource personnel, teachers, and administrators. This committee has guided the creation, piloting, and expansion of peer review ever since.

Today, Sundin characterizes the relationship between labor, management, and the district as a "very strong collaboration, with occasional glimpses of co-ownership" of the city's schools. "We are included in almost every discussion, even if it's not a labor-management issue," said Sundin. "We can focus on our common work — educating kids — rather than

---

"Teaching is the most complex job in the world. And as much as there's an art and magic to teaching, there's a science."

---

spending intelligence and emotion and energy fighting."

Lynn Nordgren, whom Sundin calls an "exemplary teacher," was on the original committee and is now the district's professional development facilitator. Nordgren believes the process is successful because it is founded on solid research from a broad spectrum of disciplines: education, of course, but also business, philosophy, psychology, and popular self-help. "We even looked at the Weight Watchers material," she said.

"Teaching is the most complex job in the world. We work with the most complex structures in the world — the human mind and the human heart," said Nordgren. "And as much as there's an art and magic to teaching, there's a science."

Jehanne Beaton, who teaches social studies and language arts, came to Minneapolis after four years in another district. "Before, I was observed three times a year. The principal would come in unannounced. It was always intimidating; I never had any input into what I wanted his feedback on or what I wanted to work on. [This process] provides me with a structure, helps me create a timeline. It's almost like it legitimizes what you really want to do. It heightens your practice."

"The PDP process is more genuine," said Scott Devens, a teacher at Floyd B. Olson Middle School. "It helps you focus on measurable results in one area. You master a little bit at a time. The whole idea is that as teachers, we have a lot to learn as well."

The plan has three tiers. The initial tier, the Professional Support Process (PSP) is for first-year teachers as well as experienced teachers with specific performance problem areas. First-year teachers work closely with a selected, trained district mentor. The mentor also helps the new teacher select a team of colleagues (including the principal) to offer support and feedback through the critical first year.

"You wouldn't have an intern surgeon do your heart bypass," said Nordgren, "without [first] observing and helping the mentor surgeon. We want to encourage people to ask for help and get rid of fears."

After year one, if a new teacher is ready, he or she moves on to the Professional Development Process (PDP) and stays at this level for the rest of his or her

---

The PDP structure — even the simple act of writing down one's goals on paper — motivates many teachers to push harder to name their goals and actively pursue them.

---

career. PDP includes setting self-directed goals and participating in at least three meetings a year with a self-selected team, composed of grade-level or department peers, other teachers in the building, the principal, and occasionally a district curriculum consultant or specialist in the teacher's field from another site. The team offers ongoing moral support and practical feedback in a collegial manner, using a variety of techniques, and also participates in the teacher's annual assessment.

If serious developmental or performance issues are identified by a teacher's PDP team, any team member or the principal can recommend a return to the more structured, three- to nine-month PSP process. The teacher's goals then become team-driven rather than solely self-directed. PSP involves a variety of strategies such as coaching, mentoring, observations, study groups, and videotaping. Upon successful completion of this process, the teacher moves back into PDP.

Finally, the Intensive Assistance Program (IAP) tier addresses the needs of the tenured teacher in crisis. IAP is a non-voluntary, confidential, six-week process after which the teacher will either move back into PSP and eventually to PDP, or will seek alternate employment. The opportunity to work with Career Options, an outplacement process involving a district facilitator

and outside career consultant, is introduced at the beginning of the IAP process. Career Options is also available to any teacher at any time.

Another facet of the Minneapolis plan is its residency program, which McRoy describes as "an opportunity for job-embedded professional development with a rigorous, standard-based approach." About a dozen Minneapolis schools have been approved as residency sites, where selected newly licensed teachers, called residents, spend 80 percent of their time in the classroom and 20 percent working on professional development with a mentor.

The residency system only functions at sites that "have a positive professional culture and support systems," cautions Sundin, so schools apply and are screened carefully before approval. "We'd love to get a requirement that every new teacher coming in would go through a residency. It gives both the district and the teacher a chance to establish whether they have what it takes to make it in an urban district. It's a mutual assessment to see if it's a good career match. We think it's the best model for induction of brand new teachers, and we will be trying to figure out in negotiations how to increase the numbers."

What the Teachers Think

Celia Burton and Rob Rumppe are at opposite ends of the spectrum. Burton teaches first grade at Sheridan Elementary School, a fine arts magnet in North Minneapolis whose 760 K-8 students are mostly lower income kids of color, including a significant number of English Language Learners. In contrast, many of Rumppe's students at Southwest High, which features an International Baccalaureate program, are college-bound and come from more affluent South Minneapolis families. Each believes the PDP structure — even the simple act of writing down one's goals on paper — motivates many teachers to push harder to name their goals and actively pursue them.

Burton admits she initially resisted PDP: "I thought it was just one more thing." But at her school, where there is near-zero tolerance for non-compliance, she says she has experienced an increased sense of collegiality, been inspired to better classroom organization, and enhanced her teaching approach.

"Last year we developed a powerful PDP plan that really affected our work in the classroom," explained Burton, who teams with other first grade teachers. "We talked among ourselves about each child, and developed interventions which guided us into writing our plan focusing on student achievement," which is, of course, the bottom line. For example, her team wants to get 80 percent of first graders reading at second grade level to compensate in advance for what they may lose over the summer.

"Because of our goals, I find myself pushing kids harder, asking them for homework every day, making an effort for 100 percent turnout for parent conferences." Of reading test scores, Burton reports, "The kids made wider gains than first graders across the district [since last year]," she said.

Rumppe, a math teacher with 14 years in the district, also wanted to improve communication with parents, so he decided to use an Internet site — accessible by student ID number — to post student grades and homework assignment status.

"I've heard lots of positive feedback," said Rumppe. "Communication is no longer limited to those who come in to the room to see how their kids are doing." And, he confesses, "It's kind of fun for parents to know the kid is missing assignments. If the kid says, 'I already did my homework,' they have the printout right there." This year, he expanded his on-line project. "I wanted to get kids to do some writing, and

post their reports publicly on the web site," he explained. Now students complete more assignments, and are more conscientious about their work, knowing others will see it. "I get the work in. And they're much more concerned about spelling and grammar," he said.

"I don't think this would have happened had I not been forced to try to identify ways I could improve communication with parents," concludes Rumppe.

"Some teachers — young and old — still roll their eyes when you mention the [PDP] word," Burton said. "But now I can't say enough about the PDP process."

Taking Risks, Breaking Barriers

Jehanne Beaton, also at Sheridan Elementary, didn't need convincing about PDP's merits. She strategically chooses her team to take advantage of experienced teachers as advisors, and to promote her ideas with teachers at other grade levels to get their buy-in. "I try to match up with critical and constructive advisors in terms of what I want to do," she notes. Her goal is to institutionalize an exit performance for 8th graders: students will read original poems, perform an original dance or piano composition, or compile a multi-media

JEAN-CLAUDE LEJEUNE

showcase of their work.

Sheridan principal Keri Felt said, "We'd had teams in the past, but they'd talk about more mechanical types of things. Their discussions were not deep and rich in terms of instructional strategies and ways they could improve themselves. Now they're getting better at it and taking more risks because they trust each other more." For example, she noted, Beaton's team risked including a parent and a student.

"The down side of PDP," observes Beaton, "is that if I wanted to, I could take the path of least resistance, and just do the paperwork. I'm lucky because I've found a school where there are lots of teachers who work very hard at creating a great classroom."

> **"We're really advocating a new belief system and a new culture that requires the Board of Education to support the 95 percent of teachers who are doing well, instead of focusing on the one to five percent who aren't."**

Creating Time for Professional Development

Site leadership is a big factor in the success of a site's PDP efforts, say participants, as is carving out the time for team meetings, discussion, study groups, and other related activities. While time is always at a premium for teachers, some strategies help. The residency program is one way professional development is built into the teacher's schedule. For example, residents at Olson Middle School meet every Monday to work on curriculum development together, while mentor teachers take the residents' classes. At Sheridan, weekly PDP meetings are calendared before the school year starts, to avoid jockeying for prep times.

The district contract also helps teachers make time for growth. It stipulates that every teacher may take two days off to observe other classrooms. And in 1987, a long-fought battle over prep time for elementary teachers — an issue that contributed to a 1970 strike— was resolved when the contract ensured that elementary teachers have the same 275 minutes of prep time each week as high school teachers.

Ushering in a New Professionalism

"We're really advocating a new belief system and a new culture," Sundin said. "It requires that the Board of Education believe in, advocate for, and support the 95 percent of teachers who are doing well, or trying to improve, instead of focusing all their time, energy, and legal dollars to try to get the one to five percent who aren't — we're taking care of [those ineffective teachers] as part of this peer review system. We're helping them find their way out of the system."

"It finally dawned on me within the last couple of months," mused Sundin, "that it's our responsibility to support the profession as a whole, not just individuals."

PDP puts a positive spin even on termination. Minneapolis Public Schools' Executive Director of Human Resources Jeff Bradt says, "This is intended to be a coaching, constructive process rather than building a file against someone. I think the primary benefit to the district is the impact it has on employees who are not experiencing performance problems. It sends a message that this is a partnership, that everyone has tools and resources to be successful."

Nordgren adds, "We've had teachers who were going to be released, but voluntarily left. They've said, 'This process was so professional. It helped me come to an understanding there are other things I could do.'"

While it is still early to fully assess the outcomes of this arrangement, the early prognosis is promising. New teachers are grateful for mentoring and support. Some criticize the process as too bureaucratic, and some say it doesn't go far enough to promote authentic staff development.

"There's great potential, but we're not there yet," said David Jones, a 24-year veteran science and math teacher, who advocates what he calls "a Japan model" where teachers divide their time evenly between classroom and collegial discussion.

Yet at the very least, most agree the district is moving in the right direction, and at best, the process has begun to raise the standard of teacher quality in Minneapolis and help students expand and achieve their potential.

The union's Audrey McRoy sums up: "There was a time when teachers kept their doors closed; it was safer. This process has opened doors. You're not doing your job in isolation. My problem may be a solution for you." **TTU**

KRIS BERGGREN IS A MINNEAPOLIS-BASED FREELANCE WRITER.

FOR MORE INFORMATION ABOUT THE PROGRAMS MENTIONED ABOVE, CONTACT: MINNEAPOLIS FEDERATION OF TEACHERS, 1300 PLYMOUTH AVE. NORTH, MINNEAPOLIS, MN 55411; 612-529-9621; FAX: 612-529-0539; WEBSITE: WWW.MFT59.ORG.

Minneapolis Contract Excerpt

Tenured teachers submit a Professional Development Plan outlining their PDP involvement, activities, and implementation timeline. The teacher also needs to select a team (of which the principal is an automatic member) and meet with that team about his/her plan. The team may then set up a timeline for further meetings as well as help with strategies and resources for the teacher's PDP plan. Tenured teachers should have, but are not limited to, three meetings annually. They consist of:

a. initial meeting to share PDP plan;
b. progress report meeting mid-year;
c. progress report meeting end of year.

In between the meetings, teachers implement their plans and utilize a variety of goal attainment techniques (peer coaching, developing a professional portfolio, observations, video-taping and analysis of a teaching session, study groups, action research, etc.) to assist in successful achievement of PDP plans.

Teachers may choose to do a variety of things to carry out their plans. Their plans are aligned with the District Improvement Agenda, School Improvement Plan goals, and the Standards of Effective Instruction. The plan must be written and submitted to the principal and the other members of the teacher's PDP team. Plans should be sent to Human Resources for placement in the teacher's file. Teachers should be sure to keep copies of everything. **TTU**

JEAN-CLAUDE LEJEUNE

Excerpted from Article VII, Section I, p. 65, from Teacher Contract, Agreements and Policies, July 1, 1997 - June 30, 1999. Minneapolis Federation of Teachers, #59. For a complete contract, visit the website: www.mft59.org.

Rochester Teachers Struggle to Take Charge of their Practice

BY CHRISTINE E. MURRAY

1987 WAS A WATERSHED YEAR FOR UNION-INITIATED school reforms, and the Rochester Teachers Association was in the vanguard of AFT locals negotiating for change. Led by RTA President Adam Urbanski, teacher negotiators successfully crafted a reform contract to reframe teachers' roles in the Rochester City School District. The contract created a Career in Teaching Program and implemented shared decision-making in all schools. Over the three-year contract, teachers' salaries were increased 40%.

CLEO PHOTO

The Rochester reforms were given high-profile treatment in the national media. Rochester's superintendent at the time, Peter McWalters, and Adam Urbanski became regulars on the education speakers' circuit, sharing their vision of reform. The contract seemed to have all the elements that school reformers were recommending to improve schools.

Twelve years later, progress has been far slower than anyone imagined. Success in changing traditional structures and roles at the district office, in schools, and within the union itself has been difficult to achieve. Adam Urbanski's aphorism, "Real change is real hard," might be the unofficial motto of the RTA.

Despite the challenges, Rochester teachers have made real progress in their efforts to take charge of their practice. The Career in Teaching Program was designed to change teacher/administrator relationships from the traditional bureaucracy to a model of peer evaluation and development. The program is jointly coordinated by a twelve-member panel, composed of six teachers and six administrators. The activities of the Career in Teaching Program are coordinated by two teachers who continue to teach half-time.

Professional expectations for Rochester teachers mirror the principles of the National Board for Professional Teaching Standards. Teachers are expected to demonstrate a commitment to students and their learning; knowledge of teaching, learning theory, and subject matter; professional development and reflective practice; and collaboration with others. The most recent contract rewards with a $1,500 salary increase teachers who successfully obtain National Board certification and who attain an evaluation of "exceeds expectations."

The Career in Teaching Program

The Career in Teaching Program outlines a professional progression for teachers beginning as Interns, and moving up a four-tiered career path with initial steps from Intern to Resident Teacher to Professional Teacher. Teachers become eligible for the fourth and highest level, a two-year renewable appointment as Lead Teacher, in their eighth year of service.

Donna Gattelaro-Andersen, a former lead teacher, offered these remarks about the value of her experience. "As a lead teacher, I was encouraged to facilitate my own continued growth as well as the growth of my colleagues. I felt valued and I had the opportunity to participate in numerous collegial activities which helped me to reflect on my own practice. Today, as a vice principal in one of our middle schools, I see myself as an instructional leader with the responsibility of reducing isolation and creating a culture which enables others to participate in continued learning."

Lead Teachers can work in a variety of roles while continuing to teach at least half-time. Selection for Lead Teachers is a separate application process. Applicants need to get references from peers and administrators, analyze and write about their own teaching experiences, and complete an interview with a governing panel. Since 1987, 420 teachers have held Lead Teacher appointments.

Lead Teacher positions are configured in several ways. Some Lead Teachers are school-based and have served either as mentors for Intern teachers or as project facilitators for initiatives, such as improving the use of technology in teaching. Depending on the assignment, school-based Lead Teachers may or may not have a reduced teaching load.

Other positions have provided Lead Teachers release time for district-wide work. In such cases, Lead Teachers teach their students in the morning. During the afternoon they serve either as mentors at other schools or as facilitators in areas such as teacher professional development. In 1998-99 there were 81 school-based Lead Teachers and 45 Lead Teachers with district-wide assignments. Of the 126 teachers, 34 had not been Lead Teachers previously.

Mentoring

In 1998-1999, all but one Lead Teacher served as mentors. This has been the case for the past three years, largely because of the high number of new teachers being hired by the district. In 1998-99, a total of 387 interns were assisted. Since the program's inception, 1,500 Intern teachers have received mentor support.

Lead Teacher/Mentors provide first-year teachers with regular classroom-based assistance, create opportunities to observe other teachers and attend professional development activities, offer regular evaluations of their progress, and make recommendations along with the principal regarding continued employment. Having more than one set of recommendations to consider has proven particularly helpful in difficult reappointment decisions. Interns also evaluate their mentors.

The mentor program has been so valuable that it has survived numerous budget cuts. Scott Hirschler, an elementary teacher now well-established in his teaching career, still regularly talks with his mentor. Reflecting on his internship year, Scott commented, "My mentor offered me a wealth of suggestions, information, and experience. But she also enabled me to find my own way as a teacher and gain confidence. That has made it possible for me to take risks I otherwise would have been unable to take. Her passion for teaching was contagious."

Reducing first-year teachers' isolation has been viewed as critically important by Rochester teachers. At the same time, the internship year provides a screening process which teachers have welcomed. Ten to fifteen percent of interns are not rehired annually. There are also interns who voluntarily elect not to continue teaching in the city, often because they are counseled out by their mentors. Of those who were

recommended to be continued after their intern year, 86% have remained as teachers in the district — much higher than the previous 60% retention rate.

This positive outcome is threatened, however, by the rapidly expanding job market in the greater Rochester area. Increasingly, new teachers who have successfully completed several years of teaching in Rochester are leaving for positions in surrounding suburban districts. Rochester's teachers' salaries are no longer more attractive than other area school districts. That, plus the fact that Rochester does not reimburse teachers for a masters' degree program, has reduced the district's attractiveness.

Teachers evaluated as "needs improvement" or "unsatisfactory" could lose their annual salary increase and are reevaluated by their administrator in the following year. When teachers take peer review seriously, it can transform evaluation practices dramatically.

Support and Intervention

In addition to working with Interns, Mentor/Lead Teachers provide assistance to tenured teachers through the Professional Support and Intervention Programs. The Professional Support Program provides peer assistance to teachers who voluntarily request help to improve their teaching. Nearly 200 teachers requested assistance in 1998-99.

Carl O'Connell, the Career in Teaching Mentor Program coordinator observed, "What we are seeing is more and more people who are asking for professional support. Ten years ago no teacher would have believed that you could call a central office number for help." The Professional Support Program has provided a formal means for teachers to assist each other in improving their practice.

The Intervention Program assigns mentors to help teachers who are having such difficulty that they have been recommended for intervention — by their principals or by their school-based planning team. The cases of teachers referred for intervention are reviewed by the Career in Teaching Panel to determine if intervention is appropriate. Teachers who are determined to be in need of intervention, but who refuse to participate, can have salary increases withheld.

Since the program's inception, 68 teachers have

been involved in intervention. Forty teachers have left the district as a result. For most, it was a voluntary separation, but there were four cases where teachers were terminated. The other 26 teachers successfully completed the intervention process.

Peer Review

The peer review process in Rochester has evolved as teachers have experimented and learned more effective ways to create a professional evaluation system. Professional teachers, who have achieved tenure and permanent teaching certification by completing their master's degrees, may participate in a peer evaluation process known as Summative Appraisal. This provides the opportunity for teachers to set their own professional goals and design their own annual assessment process. Assessment might include a portfolio of their work, peer review of their teaching, or a collaborative effort with other teachers.

Every three years, teachers who elect Summative Assessment complete an evaluation. Teachers write a report on how they have met professional standards in the areas of student learning, teaching, professional development, and home/community involvement. As part of the assessment, teachers choose two peer reviewers, in addition to their supervising administrator, with whom they complete a structured interview to assess the previous three years' work. The peer reviewers and the administrator also prepare a written report. Teachers evaluated as "needs improvement" or "unsatisfactory" in the opinion of the reviewers could lose their annual salary increase and are re-evaluated by their administrator in the following year.

When teachers take peer review seriously, it can transform evaluation practices dramatically. It supports reflection about teachers' practice and fosters interdisciplinary teaching, improved instruction, and new opportunities for students. As middle school teacher Gina Laniak commented, "I think peer review is what you put into it. If you are looking to improve yourself as a professional, it can be successful. This past year I focused on parent-teacher communication. It helped me strengthen my involvement in that area and gave me a chance to share ideas with colleagues."

A number of teachers, though, have been critical of peer review. Many observed that the paperwork required was burdensome and offered no real evidence of their teaching performance. Others felt they did not receive enough feedback, as the only formal review was every three years. Another concern was that initially, there seemed to be no consequences for minimal effort. In fact, a few teachers did not receive salary increases because they failed to comply, but this was not widely known.

As a result of these concerns, the peer review process was modified in the most recent contract and will continue to evolve as Rochester teachers gain experience with it. In their most recent contract, teachers voted to offer the traditional administrator evaluation process as an option for those teachers who prefer it. About half of the teachers have chosen peer review and the remainder have chosen to be evaluated by their administrators.

Teacher Professionalization

In many respects, Rochester has continued to be at the leading edge of teacher reform. But change has been painful and slow. Most teachers think that the reforms begun with the 1987 contract were important and necessary. They are quick to add, however, that those reforms were not enough. Teacher Donna Groff remarked, "We need more follow-up with disruptive students and options for them outside regular class-rooms, which is something the district is working on. Also, like most districts, we don't stick with anything long enough. We are always looking for the quick fix. We are such a large district that good programs get lost and we lose good teachers because the hiring practices are so slow."

Since the reform contract, the family circumstances of many students has worsened. At the elementary level, 87% of the children receive free or reduced price lunches. Student mobility rates — the number of students moving in and out of a school in a year — hover around 50%. Attendance levels at the high schools average only about 80%. Teachers often do not know which students they will be teaching from one day to the next.

Still, the 1987 contract was heralded as an educational milestone because it reflected the possibility of genuine collaboration between the teachers union and the district. More broadly, the larger community appeared to have signed on to the reform agenda in a significant way. By 1990-91 though, the alliance between the teachers and the district was fractured in a contract dispute, a conflict repeated again in contract negotiations during 1992-93 and 1996-97.

A central question in the disputes was the process for establishing teacher accountability, with the Board of Education pushing for a pay-for-performance model which teachers repeatedly rejected. Many Rochester citizens continue to hold the view that teachers are not accountable and a pay-for-performance plan is the solution. Teachers, on the other hand, often feel they are being blamed for all the problems in the schools.

While the district office organizational chart has been redesigned repeatedly over the past twelve years, support for schools to become more autonomous has been weak. Despite many successful programs at individual schools, there is no effective means to share these ideas with other schools in the district. Teachers believe that most important decisions are still made at the district office.

The employment process is a specific area where the district office retains control. Building principals and vice principals are appointed by the Superintendent with little input from the schools. While a school-based committee, including teachers and parents, has the opportunity to interview and rank teachers, appointment decisions are made by the Human Resources Department. The RTA leadership is concerned that the district's slow hiring practices result in the loss of many good candidates to other districts more efficient in hiring.

Teacher professionalization, as framed by the Rochester contract, has asked teachers to take responsibility for their practice, both individually and collectively. This has required ongoing changes for teachers and for the Rochester Teachers Association. Like other progressive unions, the RTA has struggled to assure due process for its members, while insisting that simply protecting a teacher at all cost is not helpful for children or for the teaching profession.

Rochester's reforms have survived for a dozen years in large part because of the collective bargaining process. Some initiatives have been institutionalized, others continue to be modified in response to teachers' concerns. "Real change is real hard." But the Rochester Teachers Association continues to persist in its efforts to improve the teaching profession and to support teachers' efforts to engage their students as active learners. TTU

CHRISTINE E. MURRAY IS AN ASSOCIATE PROFESSOR IN THE DEPARTMENT OF EDUCATION AND HUMAN DEVELOPMENT, STATE UNIVERSITY OF NEW YORK COLLEGE AT BROCKPORT. SHE IS CO-AUTHOR, WITH GERALD GRANT, OF *TEACHING IN AMERICA: THE SLOW REVOLUTION*, HARVARD UNIVERSITY PRESS, 1999.

FOR MORE INFORMATION ABOUT THE PROGRAMS MENTIONED ABOVE, CONTACT: ROCHESTER TEACHERS ASSOCIATION, 30 N. UNION STREET, ROCHESTER, NY 14607; 716-546-2681; FAX 716-546-4123; WEBSITE: WWW.ROCHESTERTEACHERS.COM. THE RTA ALSO PUBLISHES, *RAISING STANDARDS*, A JOURNAL THAT DEALS WITH ISSUES OF TEACHING AND LEARNING.

Rochester Contract Excerpt

1. The Intervention and Remediation component of the CIT [Career in Teaching] Plan is designed to offer all available resources to help improve the performance of experienced teachers who are having serious difficulties in the performance of their professional duties.

2. A teacher can be recommended in writing for Intervention and remediation by a building principal, other appropriate supervisor or teacher constituency of the School-based Planning team meeting as a separate group. Such written recommendation is appropriate when a teacher's performance is rated as "Needs Improvement" or "Unsatisfactory." It is expected that such recommendation shall be initiated after reasonable efforts have been made to assist the teacher. The referral for Intervention and Remediation may contain a recommendation as to a plan for remediation and indicate whether a withhold of all or part of the total next salary increase or any other action is warranted.

3. In acting upon the written referral, the Panel may avail to the referred teacher, and to the building principal and/or other appropriate supervisors, an opportunity to appear before the panel or its representatives to provide information germane to the recommendation.

4. The CIT Panel shall vote to accept or reject the referral for Intervention within thirty days of receipt of the referral and state its reasons therefor. If the Panel votes to accept the referral, the Panel shall prescribe a plan of remediation which may include, but is not limited to, assistance by a lead teacher, mandatory inservice, or other professional studies, participation in the EAP, etc. Independent of the authority of the Superintendent of Schools in Section 47, the Panel shall have the authority to impose full or partial salary withhold during the period of intervention and remediation. ...

6. The plan for remediation will be implemented under the direction of the CIT Panel. The plan will provide for the development of specific performance and professional goals.

7. Teachers participating in Intervention and Remediation will continue to receive assistance until the CIT Panel determines that no further assistance is needed or would be productive, or until the teacher in Intervention and Remediation no longer wishes to participate. The duration of the Intervention and Remediation program for any one teacher shall not extend beyond the start of one third full semester from the date of the initiation of the assistance program.

8. Teachers in Intervention and Remediation shall receive copies of all status reports and will have the right to attach and submit a written reply to the status report forms submitted to the CIT Panel by the lead teachers.

9. The CIT Panel will review all status reports and other information that may be submitted to the Panel. If the determination of the CIT Panel is that Intervention and Remediation was successful, the CIT Panel will issue a report, in writing, to the Superintendent, the RTA President, and the teacher in Intervention.

10. Participation in Intervention and Remediation is voluntary on the part of the referred teacher. If a teacher refuses Intervention and Remediation, nothing herein shall prohibit the District from proceeding with further disciplinary action after that refusal.

11. If the determination of the CIT Panel is that Intervention is not successful, the CIT Panel will issue a report, in writing, to the Superintendent, the RTA President, and the teacher in Intervention. Evaluation and/or discipline procedures, as outlined in sections of the current Contractual Agreement, may then be instituted. ... **TTU**

EXCERPTED FROM THE ROCHESTER TEACHERS ASSOCIATION CONTRACT FOR JULY 1, 1996 - JUNE 30, 2000 (SECTION 56) AVAILABLE ON LINE AT WWW.ROCHESTERTEACHERS.COM/ CONTRTOC.HTM.

Don't Sell Your Members Short

BY ADAM URBANSKI

IN PUSHING FOR REFORM, THE GREATEST RISK FACING teacher unions is underestimating our members. Anyone who thinks that teacher unions can't promote academic excellence because our members aren't smart enough, or we can't promote equity because our members are not caring enough — such people are not only dead in the water in their thinking but are harmful to the entire movement of teacher unionism.

It is also risky to confuse the view of the majority of teachers with that of the middle-level bureaucracy, which might oppose change. Reforms here in Rochester have received solid support from rank-and-file teachers, but often stern opposition from some members of the grievance committee or the executive council, who are quick to point out how things were always done in the past. What has allowed our reform efforts to move forward is that the average teacher really wants the union to promote change.

Everyone knows in Rochester that you can't use the union to hide behind and defend the status quo. Actually, that's one of the most significant changes. People have become aware that if a teacher is not doing the students any good, then the union believes the teacher is not doing the rest of us any good. We draw a sharp distinction between a teacher's right to due process, which we will defend, and using the union to get a teacher off the hook when he or she is caught in bad practice, which we will not tolerate. Our job is to ensure fairness, but fairness to all, including students.

I happen to believe this stance is also highly pragmatic. If the students do well, our members will do well. I don't believe any community will, or should, tolerate a huge disparity between the well-being of the students and the well-being of the teachers.

If teachers do not become agents of reform, they will remain targets of reform. Just because reform is difficult doesn't mean it can't be done. Actually, reform is supposed to be difficult and painful, because real change is real hard. I am firmly convinced that if

everything is going smoothly, nothing is really changing. Reformers must develop a tolerance for chaos and for discomfort. **TTU**

———

ADAM URBANSKI IS PRESIDENT OF THE ROCHESTER TEACHERS ASSOCIATION AND A LEADER OF THE TEACHERS UNION REFORM NETWORK OF AFT AND NEA LOCALS.

RICK REINHARD

Confronting Racism in British Columbia

BY TOM MCKENNA

I'M A RACIST. MY STUDENTS TELL ME SO. THEY CLAIM racism doesn't exist in our society anymore. Therefore, anyone who brings up race when analyzing injustice is a racist. According to them, I fit the bill.

I teach high school social studies in Portland, OR. Most of my students are white; so am I. Some still use the word "colored" when referring to African Americans. When I correct them, they think I am trying to be "politically correct." They are working-class kids whose experience of the world rarely extends beyond their immediate community. But they have strong opinions about the world.

When issues of race come up, a typical student comment goes like this: "It's an advantage to be colored or Black or whatever you want us to call them."

"Tell me about that, how is it an advantage?" I ask. "How do you know that?"

"I mean, just look, they get all the scholarships," they respond. "And they get hired just because they're Black, not because they're qualified."

I ask for examples. A student tells me about an uncle who couldn't get a job as a cop because he was white. I suggest that we probe deeper, that maybe we're not seeing the whole picture. "Do you really think it is easier to be a person of color than white in America today?" I question. "Do you really think there is no racism?"

That's when they lower the boom and tell me I'm racist.

After class, I talk with my student intern. We both shake our heads in disbelief and realize how much work we have to do in order to broaden our students' understanding about issues of race.

"Where do you begin with kids like these who are so far out of touch?" my intern asks. "How do you teach them about race and racism?" Her facial expression speaks volumes about the challenge of such an undertaking. We both fall into a momentary silence.

If I were a teacher in the Canadian province

Students perform at a commemoration of the Program Against Racism in British Columbia.

PETER OWENS

of British Columbia, I would at least know where to start.

A Union Dealing with Racism

The British Columbia Teacher's Federation (BCTF) has a Program Against Racism. I've been a teacher for 25 years and a member of three teacher organizations in the United States. None has had anything remotely similar.

My experience tells me that unions in this country don't have programs against racism. Unions negotiate contracts. Unions lobby for school funding. Unions back political candidates. Unions do a fair amount to support teachers but they don't focus on social justice work or on the lives of students. Yet a Canadian union, the BCTF, has had a Program Against Racism for almost a quarter of a century. How can that be?

I admit that I knew very little about British Columbia before undertaking this investigation of the Program Against Racism. Though I live only a 75-minute plane ride away, Vancouver has always felt much more distant.

Before my visit, I knew some basics. I knew that Vancouver is quite diverse (its English-as-a-second-language population in the public schools hovers around 50%; approximately 25 different languages other than English are spoken at home), and that the city has a lower crime rate than comparable U.S. cities. I had once thought about moving there during the Vietnam War. Overall, I assumed BC was similar to the United States, just a kinder, gentler version.

My first visit to Vancouver shed light on some of the similarities. I found a provincial premier mired in scandal, a large urban school district faced with a funding crisis, a newspaper decrying an influx of immigrants "who aren't appropriate for this country," and an electrical engineer from India who has to drive a cab to make a living.

My initial research about the BCTF's Program Against Racism was via the Internet. I logged onto their web page and found a wealth of information. The federation's "Lesson Aids" catalog, for instance, features everything from a Human Rights curriculum, to a Status of Women Program, to a videotape featuring noted linguist and radical commentator Noam Chomsky.

I also found the names of contact people within the BCTF. Using e-mail, I sent them endless questions about the Program Against Racism. How did it start? How does it all work? How do you get curriculum into the classroom?

Some of my questions made no sense to my BC counterparts — either via e-mail or in person. When I visited Vancouver, I asked former BCTF president Larry Keuhn, "Why go through the federation to implement curriculum?" He responded with a prolonged "hmmm" and a puzzled expression, as if to ask back, "How else would one do it?"

Rather quickly it became clear that the union is a key site for teachers to reflect on classroom issues, as well as a vehicle to address larger social ills.

The Program Against Racism isn't just a program. It is a network of committed and culturally diverse educators engaged in a prolonged struggle to fight racism in their schools and their communities. It focuses on changing the attitudes of both teachers and students, and emphasizes not only understanding racism but also taking action against it.

Many of the educators who helped develop PAR have a history of activism. Some found their lives changed by social movements in the U.S.: the Civil Rights and anti-war movements. They wanted to change what was taught in the schools and how it was taught, while building coalitions with community groups to eliminate racism. As so many PAR associates told me, they were a family. During my days in Vancouver, they let me be a part of that family. And they told me a remarkable story about a unique program.

Presenting Accurate History

In 1975, Lloyd Edwards, a teacher from Surrey, BC, stood before the Annual General Meeting of the British Columbia Teacher's Federation and offered a motion. He was concerned about issues of racism in schools. Often when he ventured into the halls between classes he saw Indo-Canadians (Canadians from India) being bullied by students of European descent. The bullied students were not finding much success in the classroom, either.

Edwards, a Canadian of African heritage, thought that teachers and, more specifically, their union should

---

One of the most refeshing aspects is that the video goes beyond an understanding of racism to trying to change racist behavior. It challenges students: "What can I do to eliminate racism, in my school, in my community?"

---

do something to address those issues. He had not organized any support for his motion beforehand. His was a solitary voice. Yet, according to many who were in attendance, he spoke with such a passion for justice that his motion was quickly seconded, a vote was taken, and, to many people's surprise, Edward's motion passed. As a result, the BCTF established a Task Force on Racism to explore the issue more deeply.

"One of the initiatives of the early Task Force on Racism was the production of a slide-tape presentation on the history of racism in British Columbia," Wes Knapp, one of the original BCTF staff members assigned to the project, remembered. The slide-tape was an attempt to come to terms with British Columbia's racist past: internment of Japanese Canadians during World War II; a provincial legislature that from 1890 to 1924 enacted at least 36 anti-Asian laws in an attempt to create a BC version of apartheid (most were overturned by the federal parliament); a generation of First Nation (indigenous) children,

separated from their families and culture while kept for up to 10 years in "residential schools" beginning in the 1930s; a long history of Native peoples' land claims lost to zealous European expansionists.

The slide-tape presentation met with stiff resistance. Two school boards banned it from their districts, arguing that "talking about racism would cause it to exist." Ironically, the controversy raised awareness about the existence of racism and a co-existent problem of denial. It also shed a positive light on the federation's efforts. According to Knapp, the Task Force on Racism's message "got out in ways that would not have normally been available." The BCTF was able to engage everyone from local school officials to community members in discussions about racism and the roles schools might play in its elimination.

"I suppose," Knapp reflected, "more than any other event, the furor around this production fueled the call for a province-wide program to combat racism."

The union was the logical organization to put the call into action. The BCTF has a rich history of social activism. A University of British Columbia student wrote a doctoral thesis about the history of the BCTF's social justice work; it was 600 pages long and did not get beyond the 1930s. More recently, the union established a Status of Women Program in 1972 to work on issues of gender discrimination. The program enjoyed strong membership and organizational support.

The Task Force called for a Program Against Racism to be established with a full-time coordinator, an oversight Committee Against Racism, an annual budget of $37,000, and a network of activists in every local throughout the province. The Task Force also understood that an activist network limited to just teachers and schools was not enough to adequately deal with the issue of racism. From the beginning, the community was seen as an integral part of the initiative.

The Task Force's recommendation was not without opposition. Some federation members argued that unions exist for the sake of collective bargaining and professional development only. Social justice, they argued, is the duty of others. But there was also considerable support and significant historical precedent for social justice work. The union held fast and, in 1977, the Program Against Racism (PAR) was established.

The real work was yet to be done. An actual program had to be built. A network of educators organized through the BCTF with community roots had to be developed. But the field work was undertaken with full support of the union. Larry Keuhn was president of the BCTF during PAR's early years and made sure the anti-racism work was not marginalized. He made it a priority to "always keep PAR connected to the rest of the BCTF," he said in an interview. "We needed to make it as central to the BCTF as it was to people's lives."

Eventually, the original PAR budget of $37,000 grew to over $300,000.

A Grassroots Program

"It was a grassroots program that sprang from all over the province," former PAR coordinator June Williams said as she spoke about PAR's early years at a recent commemoration of the program. "Teachers who lived with students daily from all segments of society, who really knew the students ... took up the fight."

"You start with a small voice and build on it," added another former PAR coordinator, Sam Fillipoff. "We built a support system and sustained it." Current PAR coordinator Viren Joshi likened the early years of PAR organizing to Margaret Mead's axiom, "Never doubt that a small group of committed people can change the world."

Staff members went out on the road, visiting local association meetings, university classrooms, and community groups. Strategies were devised to forge relationships with ethnic organizations and First Nations people (the term preferred by the indigenous people of Canada). Innovative curriculum was created and revised. "There was lots of energy around our efforts," Knapp recalled. "It was really quite exhilarating to be a part of these initiatives. They were certainly the most rewarding years of my work at the BCTF."

Former PAR coordinator Williams particularly remembers the political debates with students and discussions about racism. "Students

[were] meeting around the province," she said, "feeling they had permission to talk about this thing they were experiencing."

Curriculum development paralleled the organizing campaign. PAR created a follow-up to the Task Force's controversial slide-tape presentation, a video production, and accompanying lesson plans entitled Life Without Fear. (The video is an excellent classroom tool, as well as a valuable historical document. It can be found in the BCTF lesson aids catalogue.)

The video captures examples of conversations about racism around the province. In the conversations, students and teachers reflect upon their experience and address a broad range of related topics, such as denial, stereotypes, xenophobia, institutional racism, and social action. The lesson plans provide frameworks for analyzing the themes developed in the video and strategies for taking action.

One of the video's most refreshing aspects is that it emphasizes going beyond an understanding of racism to trying to change racist behavior. The video challenges students: "What can I do to eliminate racism, in my school, in my community?" Students are encouraged to become aware of cultural differences and the dynamics of racism, to speak out against racist comments and jokes, to ally with community members and families.

Life Without Fear's emphasis on social action reflects a fundamental PAR principle. PAR outlines four elements of a racist incident: 1) perpetrator; 2) target; 3) bystanders; and 4) interveners. "PAR

brought a paradigm shift," explained Fillipoff. "As educators we said, 'The majority of people are bystanders — let's change as many of them as we can into interveners.'"

In order to take the vision of students as informed social activists even further, PAR created Students Taking Action Against Racism (STAAR) Camps. Teacher and PAR associate Carl Beach said the camps' influence is based on the fact that "students bonded around their opposition to injustice."

Chiara Anselmo, a teacher and former student of PAR coordinator Viren Joshi, said that, this year, her STAAR camp alone will sponsor as many as 300 students from all over her region for a weekend. "We offer Holocaust seminars, human rights work, [workshops on] valuing diversity, problem solving, intervention skills," she said. "The BCTF provides the fund-

---

The Program Against Racism isn't just a program. It is a network of committed and culturally diverse educators engaged in a prolonged struggle to fight racism.

---

ing. For the first time this year, our local board will provide the transportation."

After the camps, students return to their schools and communities and create their own activist network. The camps have been well-received by students. Anselmo started with one teacher at one school. Her efforts are now joined by 11 other schools.

Teacher Workshops

From the outset, the PAR network also provided teacher conferences and workshops. Educators from all over the province were bused to a lake in northern BC for the program's first provincial training conference. "We were all strangers on that bus," said Fillipoff. "By the time we got to the lake, we were a community. It was an 18-hour bus trip.... We were together for six days, we got to see each other's warts and dimples, we built a trust which was reflected throughout the PAR network."

PAR facilitates around 100 workshops a year, with all PAR expenses paid by the BCTF. Any teacher from anywhere in the province has the right to ask PAR to come in and help, and simply has to get a commitment that 75% of his/her colleagues will participate.

Teacher commitment means a buy-in, and provides the basis for ongoing work after the workshop ends.

Through a special fund, PAR also provides money for individual teachers to implement community-based projects. For instance, a number of communities have been concerned about the impact of racist practices on the culture of the First Nations. Having been in the public system for only about the last 40 years, First Nation students were struggling in school, succumbing to self-destructive behaviors, living without much hope. PAR grants funded programs across British Columbia that brought First Nation elders into the classroom to educate a younger generation about their lost oral tradition. With the guidance of elders, high school students learned to tell their stories. Students created books and read them to elementary students. Learning took on a new light, because it was no longer solely the enterprise of an institution that had alienated First Nation people.

New Directions

At their 1998 annual general meeting, the BCTF membership voted to take the federation's social justice work in a new direction. It was decided that anti-racism work would be part of a larger umbrella covering a First Nations program and initiatives around homophobia, poverty, and the status of women.

Activists are unclear about the impact of the change. Fillipoff, like many, fears the possible loss of the network that was the heart and soul of PAR. He worries that PAR will "lose the passion and the principal focus," which he considers both satisfying and necessary "when addressing an evil like racism." He also worries that the changes "are going to return the focus [of anti-racist work] to perpetrators and victims." Finally, he is concerned because "power has been re-centered in the Social Justice Committee within the BCTF and taken out of the local networks."

PAR associate Sandy Dore is likewise afraid that under the new social justice umbrella, "all programs will be short-changed." But Dore adds that despite his fears, like most activists he supports the federation and the new direction. He is a member of the newly formed Social Justice Committee.

"The federation just can't handle a whole bunch of splinter groups," Dore said. "Putting it all under one umbrella makes it practical for the BCTF."

Larry Keuhn, the former BCTF president, also is optimistic. He thinks the new emphasis will keep the union's social justice emphasis from becoming marginalized because it won't be left up to the activists alone to get the work done. "Now, as the president of a local, you don't have a choice to say, 'I'm just interested in bargaining,'" Keuhn said. "You have to deal with issues of social justice."

In the past, Keuhn argues, when activists made social justice work their passion, it let others off the hook. It was easy for local leadership to say, "We don't have to deal with issues of race or gender — the activists are."

"A more holistic approach is necessary to make fundamental change.... Social justice is about sexism and racism, but also about many other things," Keuhn asserts. "We've not dealt with First Nations issues until now. Homophobia was never on the agenda. We cannot systematically change things by just focusing on one issue."

The consensus among PAR associates is to move on. Williams, for instance, insists: "It's not an end, only a beginning." Anselmo is busy organizing another network within the new framework. She calls it Educators Against Racism and already has over 200 teachers signed up.

If past practices offer a clue, former PAR associates will rally behind the new social justice umbrella and give it a chance to succeed. They will pave the way for a new generation of activists to carry on their work.

Commemorating and Moving On

PAR recently held a commemoration of its 24 years of anti-racist work. The last scheduled event in the two-hour long program consisted of sixth- and seventh-grade students from Vancouver who, as a result of a PAR grant, had studied with a West-African drummer. After their introduction, a cautious group of about 30 young people in the first stages of adolescence filed into the front of a large meeting room filled with unfamiliar adults. They carried a variety of drums, some almost as big the person carrying it. Their teacher said that the Yoruban song they were about to play was about respect — "respecting ourselves, learning to respect others."

A tall Indo-Canadian girl in the back row began with a single, simple beat. Others joined in, two more in the back row, then four in the front. Before long, the room filled with a poly-rhythmic

symphony. A boy seated in front put down his drum, leapt from his cross-legged position, and danced wildly across the room. Drummers shouted their support. He reclaimed his place and was followed by another dancer and then another. The audience of PAR associates and supporters stood and clapped in unison.

The music ended and the adults called for an encore. Drummers looked to their teacher. He nodded back. "OK, we will play one more song, but you have to dance." A sweeping hand gesture pointed to every adult in attendance.

Again, the drumming started with a single beat. Adults gathered in front as the rhythm built. They joined hands and they danced. Finally, they celebrated what brought them all together.

The final act of the Program Against Racism ended as it should: PAR veterans dancing in unison to the sound of student rhythms. Faced with an uncertain future, they moved forward in a collective embrace.

I watched it all unfold from a seat in the back of the room. I couldn't help but wonder what it might be like to be a member of a union that was committed to social justice; what it might feel like to be a part of the collective movement I was witnessing.

One thing was quite clear. If I remember correctly, it begins with a single voice. **TTU**

TOM MCKENNA TEACHES HISTORY AT A HIGH SCHOOL IN PORTLAND, OREGON.

FOR MORE INFORMATION ABOUT THE PROGRAMS DESCRIBED ABOVE, CONTACT THE BRITISH COLUMBIA TEACHERS' FEDERATION, 100-550 WEST 6TH AVENUE, VANCOUVER, BC V5Z 4P2, CANADA; (604) 871-2283, (800) 663-9163; OR VISIT THEIR WEBSITE: WWW.BCTF.BC.CA.

KATHY SLOANE

Staffing & Seniority in Seattle

BY MARGIE SLOVAN

SARAH SMITH, A YOUNG TEACHER AT NATHAN HALE High School, remembers when she first tried to get a job in the Seattle system. "I was really pounding the pavement," she says. "I met with seven high school principals. Most of them said they had no flexibility in their hiring."

Smith might have an easier time today. In 1997, district teachers approved a new contract which ended seniority-based hiring except in cases of layoffs and rehires, and replaced it with a school-based process. Teachers already on contract with the district get first preference over those outside.

The reform has not been without its problems and its opponents. But advocates argue that it counters a long-standing complaint of parent and community groups, and even teachers: that schools were unable to develop staffs who agreed with the school's mission and were sensitive to the needs of the students at a particular school. Ultimately, advocates argue, the reform will foster improved collaboration and collective responsibility among teachers at the school level and, in the long run, will improve teacher quality.

How the New Process Works

Any teacher employed by the Seattle school district can apply for any position in that teacher's area of certification. At each school, a hiring committee made up of teachers, staff, and sometimes parents interviews job applicants, submitting their top three choices to the principal for a final decision. Schools have some leeway with this process, as long as they hire a teacher who will help them achieve their academic achievement plan. For example, there can be various combinations of people on the hiring committee — sometimes it's only teachers and sometimes teachers entrust the whole thing to the principal because they trust his/her vision.

At Whitman Middle School, senior librarian Wendy Kimball has participated on several hiring committees. "I think the new process is a ray of light," she says. "It allows us to have some control over who is hired."

Many others agree, even experienced teachers who stand the most to lose when seniority is no longer the basis for transferring. "I've taught at schools where teachers had nothing in common with the rest of the school," says veteran teacher Doug Selwyn. "They wanted to be there because it was an easy commute." While he does not think the new process is working well yet, Selwyn supports the concept wholeheartedly. "It's really important that there be a solid and consistent match between the folks coming to the school and the school," he says.

Several months ago, the Seattle Education Association (SEA), which represents the district's 3,000 teachers, surveyed its membership about the new hiring process. "When we asked teachers if they thought the hiring process supported school goals, 80% responded affirmatively," says Roger Erskine, SEA's executive director.

It is not an easy transition, however. Some senior teachers have sad tales to tell about trying to transfer schools. In January 1998, after nine years of teaching at Hawthorne Elementary School, 28-year-veteran Garry Breitstein decided it was time for a change. At one of the new schools he applied to last year, Breitstein lost out to a man with little teaching experience. "In a situation where you're essentially equal," says Breitstein, "shouldn't my 28 years count for something?" Breitstein did find a job at another school, but he did it by bypassing the process entirely.

Third-grade teacher Fay Shimada was also looking for a new position last year. Although she had a good record and 20 years of experience in the district, she couldn't even get an interview. "I was very frustrated," Shimada says. "Why couldn't I even get through the door?" Other teachers' experiences told her why: schools were giving preference to new teachers.

Shimada amended her job search strategy. "I left off all the information about my experience, and when I graduated from school. I wanted the schools to think I was young enough to get the job."

Erskine says the union is trying to address such problems. It has suggested that schools use seniority as a tie-breaker in hiring. It has also suggested that minimum qualifications for some teaching positions include 10 years of experience dealing with urban kids.

Uneasiness with the new process is especially high in schools where enrollments have shrunk and teaching positions have been eliminated. "At my school, we feel real insecure," says John Borga, an elementary school teacher in Seattle's North End, one of the schools with reduced enrollments. "There's no guarantee when you interview for a job that somebody will find you attractive. You're competing with everybody

Advocates argue it counters a long-standing complaint of parent and community groups, and even teachers: that schools were unable to develop staffs who agreed with the school's mission and were sensitive to the needs of the students at a particular school.

else who wants to teach in Seattle."

And if you are a teacher with seniority, odds can be stacked against you, because teachers on hiring committees may not want to hire people with more seniority. "With the school populations so unstable now," says Shimada, "people are saying, let's hire someone young and new, because if there are cuts they will be the first to go."

based management.

"These things are all linked," says Erskine. "Teachers are now required to develop an academic achievement plan. There's no sense in doing that if you can't decide who to hire."

Another part of the master plan is giving schools the power to spend money, and half of the district's $346 million budget is now in the hands of its 97 schools. Each school's "leadership team," which may include the principal, teachers, parents, and staff, has control over funding school employees (teachers and staff) and supplies. The budget for food service, custodians, and transportation is still administered by the school district.

An interesting aspect of the district funding formula gives each school additional money for students who qualify for free- or reduced-price lunches, and for bilingual students, special education students, and those with low test scores. Such weighted funding formulas have long been advocated by those who argue that the rhetoric of "quality education for all" is meaningless unless extra resources are provided to students who need them the most. About 41% of Seattle's 47,500 public school students are low income, and 34% are either Asian-American or Hispanics, some of whom speak English as a second language.

As with the school-based staffing policies, the new budgeting process has not been without its problems. In particular, it requires training and time, both of which are sometimes in short supply.

Most of all, the school-based reform requires trust and cooperation in the building. That may also be in short supply.

"Our principal is unwilling to share class sizes with us," says one high school teacher. "She says the other teachers will feel bad. How can we do our budget this way? We should have a spreadsheet for every period and every class."

At Nathan Hale, meanwhile, Nick Cabot said that trust had made the budget process easier. "This is a remarkably collegial group of teachers," says Cabot. "We always manage to work things out." Experience helps too. Teachers at Nathan Hale have been doing the school budget for several years.

The trust factor also helped Breitstein's new colleagues plan their budget in one faculty meeting. "There's a sense of contentment here," says Breitstein,

While Erskine admits the changes in school populations are displacing teachers, "nobody is going to lose a job unless they're not performing." He adds that the district is facing a lack of teachers in the next few years, not a surplus. "There's always going to be jobs," he says.

Decentralization Changes

The school-based process for staffing decisions is part of a larger decentralization process that began under Superintendent John Stanford, the popular retired Army general who ran the district for three years until his death in November 1998. Stanford worked closely with the teachers union and other groups to begin initiatives that would give schools, and especially principals, more responsibility. The 1997 teachers' contract deals not just with staffing, but has a great deal of new language designed to encourage site-

now teaching 4th grade at a school in Beacon Hill. "People don't challenge the principal as much." It doesn't hurt that the weighted student formula weighs heavily in favor of his school, which has a large group of ESL and special-education students.

The union and the district have brought in the Federal Mediation and Conciliation Service (FMCS) to help schools that have no history of working together to learn collaboration skills. "We anticipated this would be a problem," says Erskine. "But I do think we're working hard to walk the talk."

Erskine estimates that about 70% of Seattle schools are having some degree of success in working collaboratively. Of the rest, about 10% are "struggling mightily," he says. The union and the district will be paying focused attention to those schools in the coming months.

Lessons for Others

The 1997 Seattle contract takes place amid discussions across the country of increased decentralization, although it varies as to who is proposing decentralization, and how much, and for what reasons. What lessons does Erskine offer for those considering increased school-based staffing and budgeting?

"If I had to do this again," says Erskine, " I would work very hard up front, building collaboration and trust between the principal and staff. Especially where the buildings have a history of animosity." He's also learned that making each school's academic achievement plan as focused as possible is key to streamlining the reform process.

"The more thought-out this plan is," says Erskine, "and the more it is shared by the staff in the building, the more focused your budgeting and staffing will be. If you decide that every kid has to have an IEP, guess what? You'll put more of your budget into hiring more people."

In the year 2000, the Seattle teachers union will vote on a new contract. Half of the union's Executive Board is against many of the current reforms and will be running a strong campaign to win control of the board.

Dave Cook is a former SEA board member who supports decentralization but is pessimistic about its future, in large part because it doesn't grapple with the issue of adequate resources for the schools.

"There's a context of insufficient funds to do what we need to do," he says, "but more and more pressure from the public and the legislature to demonstrate more and more effectiveness. It's a terrible situation to be in."

Meantime, for teachers who have the energy, it is an exciting time to work in the Seattle School District. "I do feel hopeful," says Eliza Fox, a young math teacher at Ingraham High School. "A couple of years ago there were a lot of people here who said, 'I'm here, I go home at 2:45 — that's how schools have always been and I give up.' Now there are people who don't want to accept that." TTU

MARGIE SLOVAN IS A FREELANCE WRITER LIVING IN SEATTLE, WASHINGTON.

FOR MORE INFORMATION ABOUT THE PROGRAMS MENTIONED ABOVE, CONTACT: SEATTLE EDUCATION ASSOCIATION, 720 NOB HILL AVE. N., SEATTLE, WA 98109; 206-283-8443; FAX: 206-283-1500; WEBSITE: WWW.WA.NEA.ORG.

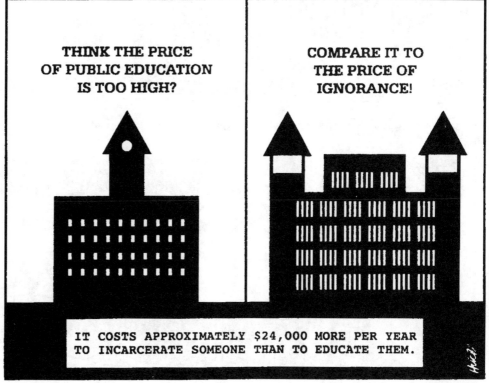

THINK THE PRICE OF PUBLIC EDUCATION IS TOO HIGH?

COMPARE IT TO THE PRICE OF IGNORANCE!

IT COSTS APPROXIMATELY $24,000 MORE PER YEAR TO INCARCERATE SOMEONE THAN TO EDUCATE THEM.

HUCK/KONPACKI, TEACHER CARTOONS

Getting Out the Message

An Interview with Union President Paulette Copeland

Milwaukee is the home of the nation's largest private, religious school voucher program. What can teacher unions do to fight voucher programs?

We have to get two key messages to the public. First, we have to let people know what good things public schools and teachers are doing — the media rarely does that. Second, we also have to let the public know that we are aware there are schools and teachers who need help and that we are willing to help them become better teachers. We have to start dealing directly with the quality of teaching. Parents need to know that we are concerned about the children. This is the only way we are going to fight vouchers. The reason why people are going to voucher schools in Milwaukee is that they've been led to believe that teachers don't care about their children.

What specifically should unions do?

It's important for us to build alliances with parents and community groups. When parents get to know us and we get to know them, we'll be more willing to help each other. We have many issues in our community that should unite teachers and parents. Union members should get behind anything that has to do with dealing with problems like welfare reform or unemployment. There are so many things that happen in the community that affect the way children perform in school.

We should also fight for staff development — it's a key thing. For example, a recent study by the Department of Education showed that only one out of five teachers feels comfortable teaching exceptional education students or dealing with diversity. Teacher unions need to fight to make some staff development mandatory because right now people who need it the most rarely take advantage of what's offered. Teacher unions needs to work with central administrators to get this kind of staff development

HUCK/KONPACKI, TEACHER CARTOONS

going. However, we should make sure that teachers are in charge of such training as we can train other teachers better than anyone else.

Has your union's peer assistance program helped teacher quality?

Our union-initiated Teacher Evaluation and Mentoring (TEAM) program, which started only two years ago, has not really been in place long enough to determine just how it has helped with teacher quality. We do know that it is responsible for the resignation of over twenty teachers who were struggling in the classroom. It has helped others improve. This may well be an indication of the type of program that is needed to improve the quality of teaching.

Why did your union recently negotiate a staff selection process that replaces district-wide seniority with site-based staff selection committees?

When I took office two years ago, I sent out a survey asking for direction from our members. One area that was of high concern was the assignment of teachers to schools based solely on seniority. The teachers wanted input into who comes into their buildings. They wanted to have school-based committees in charge of determining who comes to the building rather than having a teacher "put" into a position because of seniority. Teachers felt this would help ensure that incoming teachers fit into the philosophy of the school. This in turn would lead to a stronger teaching staff that is better able to work together on a common cause.

We've just started this process but there is lots of support for it. Our site-based committees have a majority of teachers on them and include an administrator and at least one parent. I am hopeful that it will be another step in creating quality schools. **TTU**

— *interview by Bob Peterson*

JEAN-CLAUDE LEJEUNE

PAULETTE COPELAND IS PRESIDENT OF THE MILWAUKEE TEACHERS EDUCATION ASSOCIATION.

FOR MORE INFORMATION ON THE TEAM PROGRAM OR THE SCHOOL-BASED INTERVIEW PROCESS CONTACT THE MTEA, 5130 W. VLIET ST., MILWAUKEE, WI 53208; 414-259-1990; FAX: 414-259-7801.

Milwaukee Contract Excerpt

1. All schools may expand their authority to interview teachers for full-time vacancies. This expanded authority should apply to qualified schools as defined below:

a. Existing "Innovative Schools" — Expanded interview authority shall be available to the schools which had been approved by the School Board as innovative schools and had staffing interview memoranda of understanding implemented on an experimental basis prior to the 1997-99 teacher contract. By a vote of at least two-thirds of the teaching staff, each of the following schools shall become qualified ...

b. Instrumentality Charter Schools. — All schools that become MPS instrumentality charter schools ...

c. Reconstituted schools — all schools that are reconstituted in accordance with Part V, Section R shall become qualified ...

d. Schools Meeting Educational Plan Standards — All schools designated by the Superintendent as having sufficiently developed their Education Plan shall become eligible for expanded interview authority, as described below:

a) The school submits an Educational Plan ....

b) If the Superintendent determines that the plan will lead to an increase in student achievement ... the school will be notified that it is eligible for expanded interview authority.

c) Eligible schools shall become qualified for expanded interview authority by a vote of at least two-thirds of the teaching staff.

2. At qualified schools, all full-time teacher vacancies for the following school year which are known by May 1, shall be filled through a process of school-based interviews as follows:

a. As soon as possible after May 1, vacant positions at qualified schools shall be posted in all MPS schools and facilities with a copy to the MTEA ....

b. A schedule of informational meetings at qualified schools having vacancies shall be included with the postings. The informational meetings shall provide interested teachers with information about the school's program, philosophy, expectations of teachers and special qualifications ....

c. MPS teachers who wish to interview for posted vacancies shall submit the appropriate application forms to each qualified school of interest to them, by the deadline date.

d. Teacher interviews shall be conducted by the school's interview team, consisting of an on-site administrator, teachers, and at least one parent. A majority of the team shall be teachers. Through a uniform process conducted by the MTEA Building Representative, the teachers at each school shall elect the teachers for the team. The MPS administration shall be solely responsible for providing training to all persons involved in the interview process regarding discrimination laws and other statutes and regulations that impact on how interviews must be conducted ....

e. The school interview team shall review the application forms and determine which applicants to interview.

f. Team members may attempt to reach consensus in selecting an applicant to fill a vacancy. If consensus is not reached, a majority must agree to select an applicant.

g. If the procedures described in (a) through (f) above do not result in filling a vacancy at a qualified school, the interview team of that school is authorized to select a new hire from a pool of qualified applicants approved by the MPS Department of Human Resources. The selection of a new teacher by the interview team at a qualified school shall not result in the layoff of any presently-employed MPS teacher(s) ....

h. The posting, interview and selection process described above must be completed by June 15 of each year.

3. Assignments to qualified schools shall be in accordance with the integration provision of the contract.

4. Vacancies for the following school year, which become known at qualified schools between May 2 and June 14, may be filled by the school interview team by selecting applicants who had applied to the school but who were not selected during the initial interview process ... or by interviewing teachers who will need an assignment for the following school year or a new hire as long as the selection of a new hire does not result in the layoff any presently-employed MPS teacher(s).

5. Vacancies for the following school year, which become know at qualified schools on or after June 15 (and vacancies which occur during the school year) may be filled by interviews of teachers who will need an assignment for the following school year or new hires as long as the selection of a new hire does not result in the layoff of any presently-employed MPS teacher(s).

Vacancies ... which cannot be filled with new hires because their employment would result in the layoff of presently-employed MPS teachers, shall be filled by referring teachers who need an assignment including on day-to-day status to the qualified school interview teams for an interview. If a teacher is not selected by the interview team by this process, the most senior teacher assigned to day-to-day status holding the appropriate certification shall be assigned to fill the vacant position. ▥

EXCERPTED FROM MTEA CONTRACT FOR JULY 1, 1999, TO JUNE 30, 2001 (PART V, SECTION Q). FOR MORE INFORMATION, CONTACT: MTEA, 5130 W. VLIET ST., MILWAUKEE, WI 53208; 414-259-1990; FAX: 414-259-7801.

Resisting Resistance to Change

An Interview with Local Leader Mark Simon

What are some of the reform initiatives that the Montgomery County Education Association has pushed in the last 15 years?

There are many pieces of what I would call our "quality teaching and learning" reform agenda. And it fits nicely with the school system's "success for every student" rhetoric. We've pushed site-based decision making; more rigorous teacher performance standards including student achievement measures, peer assistance and review in teacher evaluation; a focus on school climate and school level intervention as the key components in student discipline; an emphasis on peer mentoring and coaching; and a much greater emphasis on teacher staff development. But the response has been slower than we would have liked.

As President of one of the largest NEA locals in the country, what have been some of the challenges you've faced in promoting a progressive agenda for teacher unions?

We have been trying to champion reform for 14 years but there has been an effort to marginalize the union. Finally, last year, we managed to negotiate a whole new direction that really empowers teachers, makes teachers more accountable, and gives teachers more responsibilities — but it turns out to be easier to negotiate language than to implement it.

The resistance, whether from principals, the school board, or administrators, is subtle yet tremendous. From teachers, the response has been cautious support, with the cynics sitting back and saying, "This too will pass."

For example, the union has attempted to establish site-based decision making councils, which we call "Quality Management Councils (QMC)." There are expected difficulties, such as overcoming communication barriers between parents and the schools, and principal resistance based on a perceived threat to their control. But teachers, who have to vote by 2/3 majorities for a school to become a QMC school, also

have to be convinced that it will be worth their while. It has always been easier for teachers to let others control the basic conditions of teaching and learning — and then to gripe in the lounge. And the district's overall reaction is that it will go along with the reform — as long as it doesn't cost much and as long as it doesn't ruffle too many feathers.

We negotiated the establishment of QMCs in our contract last year. We have 187 schools and yet we have only 10 schools that came forward to establish QMCs in this first year. It'll be voluntary until 2002 and the implementation is somewhat slower than we had expected.

What other "reforms" were negotiated into your contract?

We negotiated the establishment of 13 joint work groups to develop proposals on staff development, peer review, and student discipline. But we also wrote language that commits the school system to a culture change that involves significant collaboration with the union, greater decision making by those closest to the classroom, and increased parent involvement. The school board signed off on the contract, but their commitment to a partnership with the union is very weak. Some of our proposals are being killed with smiles. The union championing something by itself is not sufficient. We need allies. But the work to develop those allies is huge. The bureaucracies and complex communities that exist around school systems take an almost super-human effort to change. It's not just a matter of coming up with good ideas.

How is the union attempting to overcome this resistance to change?

It will take organizing, and communicating, and winning the hearts and minds of teachers, administrators, parents, and other power-players in the system. We've been working well with key members of the central administration and some principals on teacher evaluation, peer review, and site based decision making. We brought in union leaders and administrators who have developed similar programs in Cincinnati and Minneapolis. But there is opposition among some principals. The question we face is, "Are the number of dinosaurs greater or less than the number of people who can engage with the union on these issues?" Building a strong base among progressive parents will be key.

Have you had success in working with community forces?

Parents will be key. Our contract and QMCs truly empower parents for the first time. Nevertheless, the countywide PTA has not been sympathetic to an alliance with the union. On the individual school level, there has been much more receptivity. There is a new organization of African-American parents, set up by the NAACP, that has been an alternative to the county-wide PTA in over 150 schools. The challenge is for the union to build a strong alliance with the parents that are currently least well-served by the school system, and that is parents of children of color and working class families.

How do you view NEA President Bob Chase's call for "new unionism" and increased cooperation with local education authorities?

Chase's call has been very positive, even thought the reality across the country is still much less than the promise. But what's compelling is that Chase is challenging everyone — the left and the right and everybody in between — to make the union a champion of change and not just a defender of doing things the way they've always been done.

What he is proposing is incredibly hard, however. It takes an incredible persistence for those of us in the trenches to outlast the dinosaur forces in our school systems. I also think "new unionism" is almost impossible to implement in a time of austerity. If new unionism is championed at the same time teachers are being forced to accept pay or benefit cuts or insufficient pay increases, then

It takes an incredible persistence for those of us in the trenches to outlast the dinosaur forces in our school systems.

teachers have a hard time separating the reform agenda from the cuts. As a result, union officials won't be long in office.

I'm optimistic, however, because I think there is a possibility for community support for increased funding for education. First, most states and the federal government are flush with money right now, especially if the surplus is used for social programs rather than used to justify tax cuts. It's a good time to demand more resources for schools and children.

Second, the public's attention is focused on education; people who have credible solutions are going to get a good hearing. It is a great time for unions to be championing a reform agenda. In fact, I don't think there has ever been as good a time. **TTU**

— interview by Bob Peterson

MARK SIMON IS PRESIDENT OF THE MONTGOMERY COUNTY EDUCATION ASSOCIATION, MARYLAND.

FOR MORE INFORMATION ABOUT THE PROGRAMS MENTIONED ABOVE, CONTACT: MONTGOMERY COUNTY EDUCATION ASSOCIATION, 60 WEST GUDE DRIVE, ROCKVILLE, MD 20850; 301-294-6232; FAX: 301-309-9563; WEBSITE: WWW.MCEA.NEA.ORG.

KONOPACKI
©1997
HUCK/KONOPACKI TEACHER CARTOONS - APRIL

Montgomery Co. Contract Excerpt

FROM MONTGOMERY CO. (MD) EDUCATIONAL ASSN.

The parties to this agreement believe that a quality education is a fundamental right of every child. All children can learn, and we do not accept the excuse that students have a right to fail. All of us have the responsibility to preserve the right of all students to succeed and to promote success for every student. We further recognize and greatly appreciate the extraordinary commitment of teachers, administrators, and all other school employees and the efforts they make every day to meet the needs and further the interest of students.

This negotiated Agreement was created using an interest-based bargaining process, a new process for Montgomery County Public Schools (MCPS) and the Montgomery County Education Association. It is much more than a contract that describes the wages, hours, and working conditions of the unit members covered by it. This negotiated Agreement describes a relationship of collaboration being forged between the teachers' union and the school system, dedicated to the continuous improvement of the quality of education in MCPS. For the union, taking responsibility for the improvement of the quality of teaching and learning represents an expanded role and for the administration, forging a partnership with the union over ways the system and schools can improve is also new. In effect, this Agreement becomes a compact defining how we will work together in new ways in the interest of students. We commit to work together to obtain and/or realign resources necessary to implement the goals and concepts described throughout this agreement. With this compact, we re-dedicate ourselves to a shared commitment to the goals of MCPS:

1. Ensure Success for Every Student;
2. Provide an Effective Instructional Program;
3. Strengthen Productive Partnerships for Education;
4. Create a Positive Work Environment in a Self-renewing Organization.

Continuous Improvement Core Concepts:

1. Our purpose is to achieve continuous improvement in the quality of teaching and learning for all students.

2. An inclusive, fair, and meaningful process of stakeholder involvement is essential to the design and implementation of a continuous improvement partnership.

3. A critical spirit and inquiry ethic, constancy of purpose, and learning are precursors to improvement.

4. Decisions about teaching and learning should be made by those closest to the teaching and learning process within each school community.

5. Training and human resource development are key to managing change in a continuous improvement system.

6. Leadership can be exercised by any employee, regardless of position.

7. Accountability for results will be shared responsibility. TTU

EXCERPTED FROM THE CONTRACT BETWEEN THE MONTGOMERY COUNTY EDUCATION ASSOCIATION AND BOARD OF EDUCATION OF MONTGOMERY COUNTY, ROCKVILLE, MARYLAND, FOR THE SCHOOL YEARS 1999-2001.

FOR A FULL COPY OF THE CONTRACT, SEE THE WEBSITE: WWW.MCEA.NEA.ORG/CONT.HTM.

When Collective Bargaining Is Prohibited

An Interview with Rukiya Dillahunt

North Carolina is one of a few states where state law prohibits teachers and all other public employees from bargaining collectively. Despite this prohibition, teachers are active politically, working to improve teaching conditions, salaries, and student learning. Moreover, there is a movement developing to change the law in North Carolina. The Wake Association of Classroom Teachers (WakeACT) has approximately 3,500 members representing one-half of the teachers in the system.

What is it like working in a state that prohibits collective bargaining?

It is difficult at times. Since we do not have the legal right to bargain a contract, we organize in other ways. For example, we work to elect local school board members and county commissioners who support public education. We lobby the school board and meet with the central office administrators. We try to reach agreements on issues such as transfer policies, calendar, benefits, and salaries for all school employees. Through our efforts, we've won many struggles. For example, we stopped privatization of school bus drivers and cafeteria workers.

At the state level, we help elect pro-education legislators and we lobby on issues including salaries, retirement benefits, teacher planning periods, career status, and reform issues like accountability. Because of our political power, the state legislators have agreed to raise teacher salaries to the national average. In order to defeat proposals for vouchers, we had to compromise and agree to charter schools.

The bottom line is we have to be organized, creative, and persistent.

What do you think teacher unions should fight for in the coming years?

We need to focus on educating all students. Currently, some of us have a tendency to blame parents

when students are not performing academically or socially. We can not ignore the social ills in our society and the conditions in many of our neighborhoods. But we have to re-educate and retrain teachers so they can learn to work with all the students who are entering our classrooms. We need to move out of our traditional teaching model into alternative styles of learning and schedules.

Teacher unions need to recognize and admit that the parents of students of color feel that public schools are not serving their children equitably. Nationally, there is a trend developing among African-American parents to enroll their children in charter schools and private schools. In North Carolina, 85% of the students entering charter schools are African American. We must ask why? Then rectify the problem in our school systems.

We must encourage parents of color to become full-time partners in their child's education process. They must feel welcome and part of the team. We must begin to discuss institutionalized racism and its effects on students of color.

The unions must take the lead in addressing the quality of education and equity issues in our schools. If we continue to reduce the problem of racism to "diversity" we will make it easier for the enemies who attack public education.

What do you mean by "re-educating teachers?"

Unfortunately, some of our colleagues, particularly veteran teachers, have a difficult time being flexible and changing their style of teaching. The mentality often is "I have been teaching forty-plus years — why should I change?" We put the blame totally on our clients and hesitate to assign any responsibility to ourselves and the educational system. The traditional ways are not working with the students who are coming into our schools.

The educational family must be more flexible,

initiating different teaching styles to deal with the various styles of learning of our students. Professional development is key in implementing change. Teachers must take the initiative if we are going to win the trust, confidence, and respect of our parents and students of color.

You have been known as a firm advocate of building alliances with community members and parents. Why do you think this is important?

One reason is that we need to reconnect our families to our schools. The majority of students of color are bused outside of their neighborhoods to school. The concept of community schools and community involvement is completely lost. Many parents and grandparents do not share the spirit of ownership in the schools.

A second reason is that teacher unions can use such alliances to help people understand the problems that we face within the schools. For example, most parents are unaware of how much money teachers spend out of their pockets for supplies. When made aware of this large amount, PTAs and parents are more supportive of increasing resources for teachers and schools.

A third reason is that such alliances help teachers and schools recognize and relate to the needs of the community. This means teacher unions getting involved in community struggles that might not appear to have a relationship to education. But they do. Community issues that affect families' survival are vital. When we get involved in such issues we will witness an increase in the trust level and respect by the parents and the community in general. **TTU**

— interview by Bob Peterson

RUKIYA DILLAHUNT IS THE PAST PRESIDENT OF THE WAKE ASSOCIA-
TION OF CLASSROOM TEACHERS IN RALEIGH, NORTH CAROLINA.

Lessons from History

Why Teachers Should Know History

An Interview with Historian Howard Zinn

The following is condensed from an interview with historian Howard Zinn, author of A People's History of the United States. *He was interviewed by Bob Peterson of* Rethinking Schools.

How has the labor movement contributed to the economic well-being of people in our society?

There is nothing in the U.S. Constitution that guarantees economic rights such as decent wages, or decent hours of work, or safe working conditions. As a result, working people have always been forced to act on their own. One way they have done this is through the labor movement.

Without the labor movement, for example, it's doubtful that working people would have won the 8-hour day. Not only did workers not have government on their side, the government was on the other side. All through the latter part of the 19th century and the early 20th century, the government was using the police and the army and the National Guard and the courts to break strikes throughout the country.

In the 1930s, workers organized to extend the benefits of labor organization beyond the small percentage of workers covered by the AFL [American Federation of Labor] craft unions — that is, to extend the benefits to the women, people of color, unskilled workers, and immigrant workers who were excluded from the AFL. This led to the formation of the Congress of Industrial Organizations (CIO).

A more recent example is the farmworkers organizing on the West Coast in the 1960s to bring at least a modicum of decent conditions to people who had been left out of organized labor for a long time.

It's interesting that this country boasts so much about our standard of living compared to that of people in other countries. While that's generally true, this higher standard of living did not come as a result of governmental initiative — or some action by Congress, or the Supreme Court, or the President. It came as a result of working people organizing, going on strike, facing off with police, going to jail, getting beaten, getting killed. The history of labor struggles in this country is one of the most dramatic of any country in the world.

Why do you think that today, less than 14% of the workforce in the United States is unionized?

For one thing, the history of working people and of the labor movement is not taught in this country. It's not in the school books and it's not in the mass media. So workers are unaware of past labor struggles, and this can have a debilitating effect.

It's also harder today to organize workers because of changes in the economy. Manufacturing has shrunk while the service industry has grown. But service and white-collar workers are much harder to organize than blue-collar workers in large factories. Now there is also the problem of organizing in an increasingly global economic structure.

One reason the American workforce has been so little unionized, even in its best years, has been the tensions between white and black, men and women, played upon by the employers. But also, unions themselves have discriminated against people of color and women. Look for instance, at the disproportionate number of men who hold official positions in trade unions. And often, unions have not fought hard on the issue of equal pay for equal work for women and minorities.

Then there is the intimidation factor. President Reagan broke the strike of the air traffic controllers almost as soon as he came into office in 1981, and that put a great fear into workers who might have been thinking about going on strike. Also, the National Labor Relations Board has, in recent decades, become more of a tool of corporations. Nor have the courts been quick to support workers' rights. All these factors are serious obstacles to workers trying to organize.

Have there been times when the U.S. labor movement has played a noticeably more progressive role, going beyond bread-and-butter issues for its members?

Here's one example. During the late 1930s, when fascism was rising in Europe, the progressive labor unions in the United States refused to work on ships from Germany. They also tried to establish boycotts of goods from Germany and Italy.

In the 1930s, the labor movement was farther to the left than it is today. The CIO, which later joined with the AFL, took a lot of important stands for peace and justice. There were CIO conventions where they talked about health care, job security, even basic changes that needed to take place in the social structure. This broader focus, however, changed almost immediately after World War II. The ferocious anti-communism of the Cold War led to demands that trade-union leaders take loyalty oaths and swear they weren't involved with the communist movement. It was at this time that the labor movement dropped its concern with broader issues of peace and justice and international solidarity.

If you go back to the early 20th century, you have the Industrial Workers of the World (IWW), which was more than a labor movement and which fought for the total restructuring of society. The IWW went far beyond the focus of the AFL, which was to simply get higher wages and better working conditions for its narrow band of workers. Of course, the IWW was destroyed by the government during and after World War I.

In fact, one of the functions of war is to give the

If teacher unions want to be strong and well-supported, it's essential that they not only be teacher unionists but teachers of unionism.

government an opportunity to get rid of troublesome, rebellious movements in society. The government in this country has been very good at taking the patriotic spirit that exists during war and using it to whip up hysteria and justify putting labor leaders into jail. During World War I, for instance, the government put virtually all the IWW leaders on trial, for conspiracy to hinder the draft and encourage desertion, and gave them long prison sentences. And after World War II, during McCarthyism and the Cold War, progressive leaders of the labor movement were forced out of their positions. You have to remember that the Cold War and McCarthyism were not just phenomena of the Republican Party. They were part of a clearly bipartisan effort to get rid of the radical forces in the labor movement and get rid of the larger issues that the CIO was concerned with.

What role did the labor movement play in the Civil Rights Movement?

In my experience, the labor movement was not involved in the Civil Rights Movement in the South, one reason being that the labor movement has never been well-organized in that part of the country. When the Civil Rights Movement began to act on the national level, there was a distinct difference in the way the unions responded. The progressive unions such as District 65 of the Retail, Wholesale and Department Store Workers, and Local 1199 of the Hospital Workers Union, reacted very positively and were helpful in fundraising and in giving support. There were also rank-and-file workers from across the country who supported the Civil Rights Movement.

But not all unions responded positively. For example, in 1964, the Civil Rights Movement fought for the rights of Blacks to be at the Democratic Convention, and were opposed to [seating] an all-white delegation from Mississippi. That's when Fannie Lou Hamer, a courageous African American from the Mississippi Freedom Party — the name given to the disenfranchised

Black people organizing their own political party in the summer of 1964 — went on national television and appealed to the nation. But the top leadership of the AFL-CIO — for example, then-head Walter Ruther — wanted the Mississippi people to accept a very pitiful, token representation in the Mississippi delegation. They didn't want the Blacks to even have a vote, but to just sit there at the convention.

What has been the role of organized labor in other peace and justice movements you've participated in?

During the movement against the war in Vietnam, there also was a distinct difference between rank-and-file workers and some of the more progressive unions, on the one hand, and the national leadership of the labor movement. The progressive forces were involved in the anti-war movement from the start. But the national leadership, which then, as now, was tied to the Democratic Party, was slow to join the forces against the war. It did so only when the country as a whole was disgusted with what we were doing in Vietnam.

Currently a debate rages about the role of government in society. What lessons can we draw from history?

This issue of the popular attitude toward government is very interesting. I believe this attitude is, by and large, created by politicians and the media. They have managed to take this very complicated question about the role of government and, very cleverly, make it seem like it's wrong when the government does something for poor and working people.

It's important to point out that big government in itself is neither good nor bad. It all depends on what class the government is favoring.

Remember the slogan that Clinton threw out during his last campaign? "The era of big government is over." That slogan shows how poorly people in this country have been taught our history. It is so misleading and hypocritical for Clinton to talk about the era of big government being over. For most of our history, government has been used to support the rich and the corporations. It is only relatively recently, in the 20th century — particularly in the 1930s with the New Deal and in the 1960s with programs such as Medicare and food stamps — that the government has responded to the demands and interests of ordinary people.

For most of our history, in fact from the very beginning with the establishment of the U.S. Constitution, the government has favored the upper classes. The Constitution was intended to create what we

JEAN-CLAUDE LEJEUNE

Every union has to have a constantly active rank-and-file, defending their rights every day. It's analogous to society at large, where citizens cannot just simply vote people into office and then relax.

might call big government, a strong central government, for the purpose of aiding the bond holders, the slave holders, and the land speculators.

On the other hand, when government is affected by popular movements, citizen movements, or protest movements, it is possible that occasionally the government will do something which helps the people who are in need. We have examples of government doing very good and useful things. One thinks immediately of the GI Bill of Rights, right after World War II, when government funding enabled millions of veterans of WWII to have a college education, and which democratized the educational system of the country almost overnight.

Today, interestingly enough, complaints about big government have been centered around welfare, Social Security, unemployment security, minimum wage. These are examples of where government is absolutely necessary, yet they are being attacked.

On the other hand, we have big government today in the form of the Pentagon — government contracts to manufacturers of nuclear weapons and military hardware, jet planes and aircraft carriers. That's a very, very big government involved there.

I think it's important to point out the distinction between the historically pro-business actions of the government and the occasional pro-people actions of the government.

What role could teacher unions play in terms of promoting such an understanding?

If teacher unions want to be strong and well-supported, it's essential that they not only be teacher unionists but teachers of unionism. We need to create a generation of students who support teachers and the movement of teachers for their rights.

In many cities, the teachers are mostly white and the students are mostly students of color. How has the labor movement hindered or helped in the struggle against racism?

This is an important issue. Racism has historically been used in the United States to divide white and black workers from one another. Sometimes people ask why is there no great socialist movement in the United States as has developed in other countries. One of the reasons is the division among workers. And the biggest division is the racial division which employers have used again and again. Very often, the result has been that unions have been racist. The AFL consisted of white-only craft unions, and Blacks were excluded.

On the other hand, the IWW at the beginning of the century welcomed everybody, and the CIO organized in mass-production industries such as auto, steel, and rubber, which had large numbers of black workers who had come up from the South after World War I. The CIO had to organize both white and black workers, and they struggled together during the strikes of the 1930s. That was a very positive movement in the history of race relations in the trade union movement.

But racism is a constant problem and remains a problem today. It raises the question of labor unions thinking beyond their most narrow interests and thinking in terms of larger social issues like racial equality and sexual equality. You would think that unions would be in the forefront in fighting against racism and sexism, but in fact unions have very often been obstacles.

I think progressive people who work in labor unions need to enlarge the social view of the labor movement, so that it understands that labor is most powerful when it can unite people across lines of sex and race, foreign-born, native-born, and so forth. This unity serves not only the immediate and practical purpose of strengthening the labor movement, but also speaks to the larger moral reason of doing it because it is the right thing to do.

Why do labor unions have a tendency to become bureaucratic and undemocratic?

It's for the same reasons that all organizations have a tendency to become bureaucratic. And that is: success creates top-heavy leadership, and the accumulation of a treasury creates opportunity for corruption and high salaries. Also, union leaders negotiate with employers and begin to get closer to employers than to their own members.

Labor unions aren't the only ones who suffer from this problem; it's a constant struggle in all organizations to maintain the power of the active rank-and-file. What it means is that members of unions cannot be complacent. Every union has to have a constantly active rank-and-file, defending their rights every day. It's analogous to society at large, where citizens cannot just simply vote people into office and then relax.

What do you think about labor/management cooperation for teacher unions?

It's a delicate matter because there is nothing wrong with cooperating on certain things with administrations, school boards, and administrators, as long as you don't give up the independent strength of the teachers. It's also important that teacher unions become more inclusive and include part-time teachers, service workers, librarians, and secretarial staff — in other words, to become industrial unions rather than narrow craft teacher unions. That will strengthen the teacher unions and then when they do things jointly with administration, it will help guarantee that they are not dominated by the administration in those joint activities. TTU

Resources for Teaching Labor History

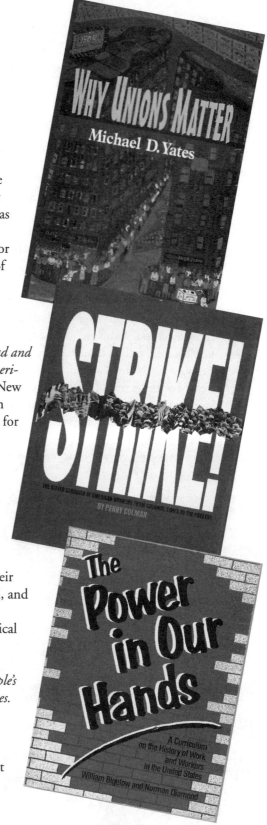

American Social History Project. *Who Built America?* (2 volumes). (New York: Pantheon Books, 1992). The central focus of this history is the changing nature of work in America. A CD-ROM on the years 1876 to 1914 is also available.

Bigelow, Bill and Norm Diamond. *The Power in Our Hands: A Curriculum on the History of Work and Workers in the United States.* (New York: Monthly Review, 1988). The best curriculum on labor history available. Role plays and writing activities help students explore issues about work and social change.

Brecher, Jeremy. *Strike.* (Boston: South End Press, 1977). A very readable general history of U.S. labor.

Boyer, Richard and Herbert Morais. *Labor's Untold Story.* (Pittsburgh, PA: United Electrical, Radio and Machine Workers of America, 1965). A lively rendition of some of the most intense labor conflicts in U.S. history. Available directly from UE, 412-471-8919.

Colman, Penny. *Strike: The Bitter Struggle of American Workers from Colonial Times to the Present.* (Brookfield, CT: Millbrook Press, 1996). An oversized book with illustrations summarizing U.S. labor history. Good for elementary grades as well as middle and high school.

Foner, Philip S. *The History of the Labor Movement in the United States* (10 volumes). (New York: International Publishers, 1982-1991). The authoritative history of the U.S. labor movement. Foner also has published several dozen other books on U.S. labor history, including a set of volumes on the history of women in labor and Blacks in labor.

Meltzer, Milton. *Bread and Roses: The Struggle of American Labor 1865-1915.* (New York: Vintage, 1973). An engaging history written for middle and high school students.

Yates, Michael. *Why Unions Matter.* (New York: Monthly Review, 1999). A clear introductory book about why unions are important, their weaknesses and potential, and their connections to the broader progressive political movements.

Zinn, Howard. *A People's History of the United States.* (New York: Harper and Row, 1995). The best single-volume history of the United States. A must for any teacher of social studies of any kind. **TTU**

The Chicago Teachers' Federation and Its Legacy

BY ROBERT LOWE

MOST EDUCATORS HAVE LITTLE FAMILIARITY WITH teacher unions and their major leaders in the era before collective bargaining. There certainly are no household names like Albert Shanker from that period. Yet one leader from the early 1900s has approached iconic status among historians since David Tyack wrote about her in *The One Best System* a quarter century ago. Dubbed as one of the "lady labor sluggers" by a prominent enemy, Margaret Haley was an enormously capable, courageous, and charismatic figure. Along with the less public though perhaps strategically more brilliant Catherine Goggin, Haley headed the Chicago Teachers' Federation (CTF), which was both a women's organization and the first group to militantly seek better conditions for teachers. The story of the CTF's exploits has been retold in a number of scholarly works that view it as devoted to greater democracy both inside and outside the schools.

Although historians essentially have limited their focus to the struggles between the CTF and the Chicago elite, at least implicitly they have viewed the activities of the CTF as benefiting not only teachers, but also students, especially those from working-class backgrounds. Haley herself eloquently maintained that the work of organized teachers would necessarily benefit students. "There is no possible conflict between the interests of the child and the interests of the teacher ... ," she claimed. "For both the child and the teacher, freedom is the condition of development. The atmosphere in which it is easiest to teach is the atmosphere in which it is easiest to learn. The same things that are a burden to the teacher are a burden also to the child. The same things which restrict her powers restrict his powers also."[1]

The conviction that furthering the interests of teachers will serve the interests of students has been a mainstay of thinking about organized teachers' activities from Margaret Haley's day to our own. Yet this essay will suggest that the interests of the CTF did at times conflict with those of students. An examination of both the accomplishments of the CTF — which most historical treatments have emphasized — and its questionable educational stances has potential implications for reconsidering the purposes of teacher unions

JEAN-CLAUDE LEJEUNE

today.

In the late 19th century, urban elementary school teachers, though better off and better trained than rural teachers, faced daunting conditions. They met classes that had as many as 70 students of varying ages who spoke a multitude of languages, and they were compelled to carry on instruction in dark, grim, often malodorous classrooms. Wages were low, retirement benefits non-existent, and job security precarious. In Chicago, the passage of a first, frail pension law inspired the creation of the Chicago Teachers' Federation, which organized initially to defend and expand it. Thereafter, the CTF dedicated itself foremost to the improvement of teachers' material conditions. Underscoring this emphasis, its constitution stated, "The object of this organization shall be to obtain for teachers all the rights and benefits to which they are entitled."[2]

The demand for rights and the active pursuit of better working conditions violated dominant assumptions about women's proper conduct. Such assertiveness was viewed as particularly unseemly by an establishment that expected teachers to be docile and to virtually take vows of poverty. In response to the CTF's effort to increase salaries, for instance, the *Chicago Times Herald* chastised the organization for "a spirit not creditable to a standard of professional ethics."[3]

Challenging the Power Elite

Undeterred by such criticism, Haley launched one of the exploits for which the CTF would become most famous. As a result of prodding from the CTF, the school board agreed to a new salary schedule that provided raises for teachers in the eighth, ninth, and tenth years of service. Two years later, however, the board abolished the new schedule, pleading lack of funds. Rather than accept the board's financial situation, the CTF investigated why the coffers were empty and found that many corporations were not paying their fair share of taxes to the city. The CTF proceeded to take the utility companies to court, and it won. The companies were required to pay approximately $600,000 annually, of which $250,000 went to the school board. Yet the board spent this money on building repairs and coal, again compelling the teachers to take legal action which ultimately enforced the raise.

The school board was closely connected to a corporate elite that through legal and extra-legal means contributed far less than its share of tax dollars to public education. The board not only made no effort

to collect taxes owed the public schools, it also actively shortchanged the schools by asking for too little rent on property it owned. The most glaring case of this was that of the Chicago Tribune Company. With its attorney strategically placed as chair of the school board, the Tribune was given a lease free of property reassessments for eighty years.

Stinginess toward teachers and generosity toward corporations provoked the CTF to correct this imbalance. There ensued, as a number of scholars have pointed out, a kind of class conflict for which the CTF prepared by making the unprecedented move of formally allying with the Chicago Federation of Labor (CFL) and by hiring both Catherine Goggin and Margaret Haley as full-time organizers for the teachers' union. This conflict extended from battles over taxes and wages to efforts to restructure the Chicago Public Schools. The CTF, for instance, strongly opposed the report of the mayor's Educational Commission. Informally named the Harper report after Nicholas

> *"There is no possible conflict between the interests of the child and the interests of the teacher ... ," Haley claimed. "For both ... , freedom is the condition of development. The atmosphere in which it is easiest to teach is the atmosphere in which it is easiest to learn."*

Rainey Harper, the president of the Rockefeller-funded University of Chicago, the document represented the thinking of elite reformers who wanted to reduce the size of the school board and dramatically increase the power of the superintendent, making him responsible for hiring and evaluating teachers, as well as for the program of studies.

Teacher Activism

The women teachers were antagonized both by Harper's opposition to pay raises when he was on the school board and by the report's suggestion that male teachers might be paid more than females to attract them to teaching. More important, the teachers objected to centralization and bureaucratization that, they claimed, left no voice for the teachers themselves. The CTF, in fact, was a strong supporter of councils that would give teachers a voice in educational policy, and Haley, in her now famous speech before the National Education Association in 1904, opposed the de-skilling she felt would result from enacting the agenda of reformers. She warned of "the increased tendency toward 'factoryizing education,' making the teacher an automaton, a mere factory hand, whose duty it is to carry out mechanically and unquestioningly the ideas and orders of those clothed with the authority of position, and who may or may not know the needs of the children or how to minister to them."[4]

For nearly two decades the CTF successfully turned back efforts to centralize the school system. The organization also played a leading role in defeating legislation that would have created a dual system of education that in essence would funnel working-class children into a separate system of vocational education following the sixth grade.

Haley and the CTF, in addition, were active in supporting other groups of teachers to exercise voices independent of school administrators. Through correspondence, speaking engagements, setting up headquarters at meetings of the National Education Association, and forming a national organization of classroom teachers, the CTF not only stimulated a more militant disposition among many urban classroom associations, but also pushed the National Education Association — an organization hitherto dominated by male superintendents and college presidents — to address the concerns of the female classroom teachers. CTF activism played a major role in getting Ella Flagg Young elected as the first woman president of the NEA, in establishing the Department of Classroom Teachers, and in pushing the NEA to take seriously teachers' interest in better salaries, adequate pensions, and tenure, as well as to support suffrage for women. Haley, in fact, was a leader of the suffrage movement in Illinois, and the CTF took a variety of progressive stances on matters beyond the schools, including supporting striking mine-workers and advocating both public ownership of utilities and child labor laws.

Repression Against the Union

The women teachers of the CTF, then, influenced a variety of efforts and for a time even shaped a school board membership congenial to their interests. But they also made formidable enemies among the powerful. In 1915 these interests decisively struck back when the school board enacted the Loeb Rule. Jacob Loeb, a prominent realtor, pushed through a measure directed specifically at the CTF that allowed the board to fire teachers who belonged to organizations that either were affiliated with labor or had paid staff members. Subsequently, 68 educators were dismissed, 38 of them members of the CTF, including all eight officers. Most of these 38 teachers had excellent or superior ratings. All of them had at least satisfactory ratings. The CTF paid their salaries and resorted to the courts to correct what obviously was a punitive strike by the board. The Illinois Supreme Court, however, ruled that the board had acted legally, that it could deny employment to anyone, "and it is immaterial whether the reason for the refusal to employ him is because the applicant is married or unmarried, is of fair complexion or dark, is or is not a member of a trade union or whether no reason is given for such refusal."[5]

The upshot of the school board's attack on the CTF was its formal disaffiliation from both the Chicago Federation of Labor and the newly formed American Federation of Teachers. The dismissed teachers were reappointed, but some historians argue that the organization thereafter lost its social vision. The CTF, however, remained the most powerful teacher organization in Chicago for some time and with varying results opposed major educational initiatives by the school administration. Most notably, it successfully resisted the introduction of platoon schools, primarily an efficiency measure originating in Gary, Indiana, that would departmentalize instruction for elementary school children and maximize the number of students in each school by utilizing all rooms at all times.

Still a force to contend with after the Loeb Rule, the CFT nonetheless had been permanently weakened. In order to remain viable, it not only at least formally broke with labor, it also conceded to centralization of the school system in exchange for tenure, and it twice supported for mayor the corrupt William Hale Thompson, whose school boards plundered the school system. Although as late as 1928 the educational scholar George Counts maintained that the CTF was "the most influential, the most militant, and the most formidable" of the teacher organizations in Chicago, over time it lost membership.[6] Before Haley's death in 1939, the recently formed Chicago Teachers' Union (CTU) included the majority of teachers. By 1950 the membership of the CTF had declined to about 300 as opposed to 8209 in the CTU.[7] No longer a viable organization by mid-century, the CTF had left an important legacy of struggle. Counts summarized its efforts during its heyday: "This organization, claiming a membership of five or six thousand elementary school teachers and led by the dynamic personality of Miss Margaret Haley, has become a real force in Chicago politics. It has born the brunt of numerous battles in behalf of the teachers. It has fought for pensions, salaries, and tenure; it has challenged in the courts the legality of the Tribune lease of school property; it has waged an aggressive warfare against the alleged evasion of school taxes by powerful corporations; and it has bitterly opposed the abolition of the teachers' councils, the establishment of the platoon system, and the tendency toward a hierarchic organization of the professional staff."[8]

Limits to Accomplishments

Yet there were limits to what the CTF could achieve. As historian Marvin Lazerson has pointed out, the work of the CTF did not protect the schools from the inordinate retrenchment they faced in Chicago during the 1930s, did not significantly change the way corporations were taxed, did not forge a permanent alliance between teachers and labor or make the NEA more democratic or give teachers a real voice in running schools.[9] Haley, acknowledged Lazerson, "was larger than life. She was a person of enormous competence who walked — swaggered is probably more accurate — across American education at the height of

its reformist period. But she was also a person whose accomplishments and hopes were blunted time after time."[10] For Lazerson, the explanation for her failures did not lie either in the inadequacies of her leadership — which some have viewed as dictatorial — or initially at least in an ideological gap between the CTF leadership and its more docile and conservative membership. Instead he believed that Haley and the CTF were overpowered by the corporate elite they antagonized. There is certainly much truth in this perspective, and it would account for the compromises the CTF began to make after the Loeb Bill was enacted and its leaders were dismissed. But in addition, according to Lazerson, the CTF not only succumbed to greater political power, but also over time its members caved in to the ideological hegemony of elites, accepting a view of themselves as credentialed professionals whose proper domain was the classroom

rather than the wider world of class politics. As a result, the activist bent of Haley became increasingly irrelevant to the teachers of Chicago and other cities, and teachers would not again contest for power until the collective bargaining era of the 1960s.

Impact on Students

Although historians differ in accounting for the decline of the CTF's influence and its descent from a visionary program, its activities before 1916 are viewed as almost sacred. This certainly makes sense, for in its inspiring David-and-Goliath conflict with corporations and elite professionals, the CTF for a time won greater resources for the schools and resisted incursions into teachers' autonomy, while it fought for egalitarian causes beyond the schools. In pursuing this agenda, the CTF defied a definition of professionalism for school teachers that equated impecuniousness and docility with putting students first. Yet the impact on students of the enlightened trade-unionist orientation of the CTF remains out of focus because the desire to serve students was not the direct cause of the CTF's activities and the extent to which the consequences of such activities benefited students remains a question.

When Haley maintained, "There is no possible conflict between the interests of the child and the interests of the teacher ... ," most teachers suffered meager salaries, insecure jobs, little hope for a comfortable retirement, and radically circumscribed curricular and personal freedom. In such a context, her pro-

nouncement that furthering teachers' interests would further those of students appears incontrovertible. But even the Chicago Teachers' Federation sometimes pursued its interests in ways that at best were of questionable value for students. In particular, it resisted higher educational qualifications for the teaching staff. This was no trivial matter. At the time the CTF was established, the requirements for becoming a teacher were modest indeed, and the quality of instruction left much to be desired.

Pedagogical Woes

Joseph Mayer Rice's powerful expose of wretched, mechanical teaching in the 1890s has been credited with ushering in a more child-centered pedagogy that would become known as the progressive education movement. Though critical of educational work in many cities, he viewed teaching in Chicago as among the worst. There, he said, "Some of the teaching was by far the most absurd I have ever witnessed."[11] He complained of dull, monotonous instruction in the lower grades where "The busy-work consists largely of copying words either from a book or from the board."[12] Though instruction almost exclusively focused on literacy skills in the early years, he found that students generally were poor readers and writers.

Work in the subject areas also was often pitiful. A fourth-grade geography class he observed was exclusively devoted to drill on facts about New England. The teacher responded to children with phrases like "You wasn't smart that time" and "You wasn't quick enough." To Rice she said, "Some of the pupils get 'flustrated' when they recite."[13]

But what Rice found most outrageous was a technique in reading common to a number of Chicago schools. Students would begin by doing mouth exercises as a group, followed by tongue and head exercises. The children would then read — often the same passages over and over — with grotesquely exaggerated expressions they learned from their exercises.[14] The problem, felt Rice, was a lack of

SUSAN LINA RUGGLES

adequately trained teachers. He complained of the absence of educational requirements for entry to teaching and maintained that one year of high school was sufficient training to pass the teacher examination. In fact, a passing mark, along with the obligatory support of a local politician, would result in placement as a cadet who would receive a regular appointment after several months of working in the classroom.[15] Deploring the political nature of hiring and retaining teachers, as well as criticizing inadequate training, Rice maintained that "Unless something energetic is done toward educating the present staff, no material improvement of the public schools of Chicago can reasonably be expected for many years."[16]

Rice was a muckraker, and he was likely prone to accentuate the negative, but the politics that surrounded teaching opportunities and the weak educational backgrounds of most Chicago teachers were facts. These facts, however, meant little to the Chicago Teachers' Federation. It opposed increasing the educational requirements for teachers and altering the traditional way they were hired. The CTF, for instance, rejected the recommendation of the Harper report that entry-level teachers should have professional training. Yet the report did not demand that elementary school teachers acquire a college degree, as some historians have contended.[17] Such a requirement clearly would make it impossible for most daughters of working-class families to enter teaching. Rather, the recommendations were more modest. A bachelor's degree was one way of meeting certification, if accompanied by "at least nine months' study of the history, principles, and practice of teaching ...."[18] But the standard could also be met through attaining a normal school certificate or through four years of successful teaching experience.

The CTF, implicitly reaffirming the political nature of the hiring process, strongly opposed both the Harper report's recommended educational requirements for teachers and its proposal to centralize, in the hands of the superintendent, the authority to oversee the hiring of teachers. While it is possible to see the stance of the CTF as a reaction to a commission whose overall orientation was thoroughly anti-teacher, this simply was not the case. The commission's report supported both tenure after a two-year probationary period and teacher councils that would report directly to the school board.

Teachers Versus Students

The CTF subsequently continued to resist higher educational requirements for teachers. It opposed, for example, a merit-pay scheme that required teachers to take six courses in order to increase their pay after seven years of service. On this issue the teachers ran afoul of social reformer Jane Addams, who had been appointed to the school board through the influence of Margaret Haley, but who believed that additional formal education would enhance teaching capacity. Addams opined that she simply could not win the assent of the CTF no matter what adjustments the school board was willing to make: "Certainly a plan to retain the undoubted benefit of required study for teachers in such wise as to lessen its burden, and various schemes devised to shift the emphasis from scholarship to professional work, were most impatiently repudiated by the Teachers' Federation ...."[19]

The CTF subsequently continued to resist higher educational requirements for teachers.

All the CTF allowed was that the board create institutes and extension courses for the purpose of professional development. "Institute work" it stated, "under certain limits should be obligatory. Extension work should be optional ...."[20] But the organization made it totally clear that years of service alone should determine salary.[21] Using a strategy similar to present-day teachers' tendency to fulfill course-taking obligations by enrolling in irrelevant and undemanding inservice courses, the CTF for a time circumvented the spirit of this requirement by making an arrangement with the Art Institute that would enable them to take all six courses within a period of several months.

CTF members understandably felt they were entitled to higher salaries without having to suffer the burden of additional qualifications. Haley captured their sentiments when she stated that "teachers, with other workers, are not receiving a share of the public wealth proportionate to the service they render in producing that wealth .... We therefore protest against any attempt to fix salaries by promotional tests or in any way which does not recognize these fundamental facts."[22] In addition, a distrust of arbitrary authority in the hands of administrators made understandable the CTF's demand that once hired "all further advancement and promotion should be based solely on years of efficient experience," with efficient teachers defined as "all teachers against whom no charge of efficiency or unfitness has been proven."[23] Yet it is not clear how these stands were likely to improve the education of children.

The *Bulletin of the Chicago Teachers' Federation*, which Haley edited, characterized the CTF's activities as those of democracy struggling against plutocracy. There is much truth in this, given that its opponents represented Chicago's elite, given that the CTF had strong working-class support, and given that, as historian Robert Reid has pointed out, the leaders of the CTF understood that "There could be ... little improvement in the schools unless proper material conditions protected the teacher."[24] What is perhaps most remarkable about the CTF is that its democratic rhetoric proved to have substance in concrete egalitarian positions it took. These include the CTF's opposition to a separate system of vocational education — however much that opposition was rooted in the fear of a loss of jobs for female teachers — and its support for the Chicago Federation of Labor's stand against I.Q. tests, which had no material payoff for teachers.

On the other hand, the CTF at times pursued its interests in ways that neither advanced democracy nor

---

In order to remain viable, the CTF not only at least formally broke with labor, it also conceded to centralization of the school system in exchange for tenure, and it twice supported for mayor the corrupt William Hale Thompson.

---

good education. For instance, it joined labor in opposition to the establishment of junior high schools based on the legitimate fear that they were being designed to track working-class kids into vocational programs. But sustained opposition to these schools, after it became clear that this fear was unwarranted, yielded no egalitarian or educational benefit. In fact, the union mostly was trying to protect the jobs of older, less-educated teachers who did not qualify to teach in the junior high schools.[25] And the CTF's opposition to higher educational qualifications for teachers and its contention that any teacher rated higher than unsatisfactory was good enough to remain in the school system, seriously compromised teachers' potential to provide students with the demanding, Deweyan approach to democratic education that it officially espoused.

Class Versus Race

Although the CTF's close connection with organized labor encouraged it to oppose broad policies like platoon schools, a dual educational system, and

intelligence testing that potentially were biased against working-class children, this class solidarity raises troubling questions about race. Historians have been silent, for example, about whether there were any African-American members of the Chicago Teachers' Federation or whether the CTF had anything to say about Black students. Yet the teachers' long-time ally, the CFL, comprised local unions that either officially excluded Black laborers or segregated them into powerless auxiliaries. This often meant that jobs were closed to Black workers — unless they crossed picket lines during strikes, further inflaming racist feelings against them. During the 1905 teamsters' strike, race hatred was not only directed toward strikebreakers. "Unlike the stockyards strike of eight months before," according to historian William Tuttle, "the hostility of striking whites toward strikebreaking Negroes had been generalized into hatred for the black race as a whole; any Negro was a potential target."[26] Only the terrible racial conflagration of 1919, in which members of Irish athletic clubs played an especially prominent role, would be worse than the race riots that developed during the teamster strike.[27]

The schools too were not immune to this outpouring of racial antipathy. Tuttle noted that "Perhaps there was no better example of white solidarity during these turbulent weeks than the sympathy strike conducted by hundreds of grade-school students."[28] While there is no reason to think the CTF or any of its members was directly involved in fomenting the student strike, there is little reason to believe it attempted to discourage the white students or labored to provide a safe learning environment for African-American students. Led by teachers of Irish ancestry and with a membership composed of many of the same, the efflorescence of white nationalism could easily have infected many in the CTF. We do know that a lead article in the journal which Haley edited expressed solidarity with the striking teamsters, peremptorily dismissed "the question of the negro's equal right to work," and blamed the riots on both the "plutocrats" and African Americans who were described as "strange" and "irresponsible."[29]

Beyond Trade Unionism

To be critical of the CTF is not to insist that it easily could have devoted itself to creating highly qualified teachers or promoting racial equality. That it was able to wage a battle against wealth and power with some success was in itself extraordinary at the turn of the century. Yet despite its support for a number of good causes beyond the schools and its opposition to some deleterious reforms within the schools, it prefigured the limitations of contemporary teacher organizations by developing a trade-union mentality that focused too narrowly on protecting jobs, raising wages, and limiting effort. In keeping with that mentality it adopted an oppositional stance to virtually all educational reforms, regardless of merit — a hallmark of teacher unions ever since. While this resistance typically has been directed against reform initiatives from the top-down, in the collective bargaining era it also has meant resistance to efforts to achieve equality of educational opportunity through school desegregation and community control.

A number of historians and scholars of contemporary teacher unions take delight in the trade-union approach organized teachers have taken, not only for the working-class solidarity it suggests, but also for its direct flouting of an ethos of professionalism which school leaders have used to encourage teachers to become apolitical beings, devoted exclusively to their own classrooms. Referring particularly to the CTF, one historian went so far as to say, "The gimmick of reminding teachers that the enterprise of education was ultimately for the children would no longer hold these inspired women back."[30]

But education *is* for children. The problem with a trade-union approach to teaching is that it does not take the children into direct consideration at all, and what is good for teachers often is not good for students. In order to serve all students well, what is needed is a new kind of unionism that rejects both an elite-defined professionalism and a pure bread-and-butter approach that tries to maximize wages and benefits while it minimizes effort. This unionism must be grounded in a professional ethos that recognizes and responds to the claims of kids and particularly the claims of communities of color that have been poorly served by public schools. Such an ethos can guide organized teachers to take stands for just, egalitarian, and intellectually engaging schools that are "for the children." It also can create solidarities and satisfactions for teachers that current unions frustrate. **TTU**

___

ROBERT LOWE IS A PROFESSOR OF EDUCATION AT NATIONAL-LOUIS UNIVERSITY. HE IS CURRENTLY WORKING ON A SOCIAL HISTORY OF TEACHERS.

Footnotes

1   Margaret Haley, "Why Teachers Should Organize," National Education Association, *Journal of Proceedings and Addresses*, 1904, p. 146.

2   Minutes of the Chicago Teachers' Federation, April 15, 1900, p. 36, Chicago Teachers' Federation Papers, Chicago Historical Society.

3   Mary J. Herrick, *The Chicago Schools: A Social and Political History* (Beverly Hills: Sage Publications, 1971), p. 94.

4   Margaret Haley, "Why Teachers Should Organize," p. 148.

5   Robert Louis Reid, "The Professionalization of Public School Teachers: The Chicago Experience, 1895-1920," Ph.D. diss., Northwestern University, 1968, p. 192.

6   George Counts, *School and Society in Chicago* (New York: Harcourt, Brace, 1928; reprint edition, New York: Arno Press, 1969), p. 330.

7   Herrick, *The Chicago Schools,* pp. 243, 291.

8   Counts, *School and Society in Chicago,* pp. 330-331.

9   Marvin Lazerson, "Teachers Organize: What Margaret Haley Lost," *History of Education Quarterly* 24 (Summer 1984): 364.

10   Ibid.

11   Joseph Mayer Rice, *The Public School System of the United States* (New York: The Century Co., 1893), p. 170.

12   Ibid.

13   Ibid, pp. 172-173.

14   Ibid, pp. 176-182.

15   Ibid., p. 167. For political sponsorship, see Herrick, p. 74.

16   Rice, *The Public School System of the United States*, pp. 15, 183.

17   For instance, Marjorie Murphy claims that the report required "a college education of all teachers..." *Blackboard Unions: The AFT and the NEA, 1900-1980* (Ithaca: Cornell University Press, 1990), p. 28.

18   William R. Harper, Chair, *Report of the Educational Commission of the City of Chicago* (Chicago, 1899), p. 58.

19   Jane Addams, *Twenty Years at Hull House* (New York: Macmillan, 1910), p. 335.

20   Minutes of the Chicago Teachers' Federation, May 19, 1906, p. 129.

21   Ibid., p. 128.

22   Ibid., September 13, 1902, p. 4. According to the minutes, this is a paraphrase of Haley's statement.

23   Ibid., January 14, 1905, p. 91 and December 20, 1904, p. 86.

24   Robert L. Reid, ed., *Battleground: The Autobiography of Margaret A. Haley* (Urbana: University of Illinois Press, 1982), p. 34.

25   See Herrick, p. 148. Also, for a thorough discussion of the Chicago Federation of Labor's opposition to junior high schools, see Counts, *School and Society in Chicago*, pp. 167-177.

26   William Tuttle, "Labor Conflict and Racial Violence," *Labor History* 10 (Summer 1969): 415.

27   Eileen M. McMahon, *What Parish Are You From? A Chicago Irish Community and Race Relations* (Lexington: University of Kentucky Press, 1995), pp. 122-123.

28   Tuttle, "Labor Conflict," p. 416.

29   *Chicago Teachers' Federation Bulletin*, May 19, 1905, p. 1, Chicago Teachers' Federation Papers, Chicago Historical Society.

30   Murphy, *Blackboard Unions*, p. 62.

LESSONS FROM HISTORY   85

If Not Now, When?

BY DAN PERLSTEIN

AMERICAN TEACHER UNIONISTS HAVE AT TIMES joined with working-class community activists in a common battle to win more equitable and democratic schooling for all children. At other moments, teacher unionists have defended the centralized administration of schools against activists demanding community involvement in educational affairs. Unions both have been active participants in efforts to promote racial and gender equality and have opposed such initiatives. In a society marked by profound social divisions, notions of social justice in education are inevitably as varied as those proposing them. Visions of social justice, moreover, reflect a mixture of self-interest and ideological commitment. Amid all the competing ideals buffeting schools and the teachers who work in them, unionists' interpretations of self-interest and visions of social justice have themselves fluctuated and evolved.

In no city have the varied ideologies and alliances of American teacher unionism been more visible than in New York, and no city has played a more prominent role in the history of teacher organizing. Throughout the 20th century, New York has been a caldron of progressive social, intellectual, and political movements, a climate that has nurtured and enlarged the visions of unionists. Life in the epicenter of American teacher unionism has been in many ways atypical of conditions in the rest of the United States. Still, focusing on exceptional moments in American teachers' history can illuminate the obstacles to the pursuit of social justice teacher unionism as well as its richest potential.

Unionism, Professionalism, and Gender Equity

Teacher unions arose at the beginning of the 20th century, when schools responded to the class and ethnic conflicts of America's burgeoning cities with new mechanisms of centralized governance and administration, new bureaucratic procedures to sort students and divide work, and new forms of technical

and professional knowledge to guide educators. As historian Marjorie Murphy demonstrates, reformers hoped to isolate teachers, most of them women, from the working-class communities in which they taught, to win teachers' allegiance to male central-office professionals, and thus to have schools help maintain order in America's fractious cities.[1]

Teachers were torn between old allegiances and the promise of a new professionalism. Unlike Chicago, where elementary school teacher Margaret Haley led a militant, community-based campaign that forced corporations to pay their school taxes and won a pay raise for teachers, leading New York teacher unionists shared the professional aspirations of elite reformers. The United Federation of Teachers (UFT) traces its history to the Teachers Guild and the Teachers Union, inheriting from the two earlier organizations both its status as Local 5 of the American Federation of Teachers and its commitment to professionalism. The Teachers Union (TU) was organized in 1916. Union founder Henry Linville possessed a Harvard Ph.D., and over the years, as the UFT notes on its web page, top teacher unionists included "Ph.D.'s, accountants and even lawyers — men like Jules Kolodny, Dave Wittes and Charles Cogen."[2]

The male-dominated Teachers Union showed little interest in gender equity. At the same time as the TU struggled to attract a handful of teachers to unionism, New York's Interborough Association of Women Teachers, under the leadership of deputy-superintendent Grace Strachan, organized 14,000 women teachers with demands for equal pay.[3] As in Chicago, commitment to the social justice ideal of gender equity served the self-interest of most teachers.

Acceptance of male privilege and insensitivity to women's concerns have been ongoing issues in teacher-union politics. Although as early as 1925, women comprised 50% of the TU Executive Board, and in the 1930s, they outnumbered men at union meetings, when Henry Linville's ideological descendants founded the United Federation of Teachers, New York organizers once again ignored women teachers as potential unionists. "When teachers loudly and publicly bicker with each other, when tongue-clucking 'talk' and futile hand wringing are substituted for vigorous action," UFT president Charles Cogen argued in urging teachers to abandon other organizations, "how can we expect anything but contempt?" Cogen labeled an "old woman" a teacher "of any sex or age who ... accepts unquestioningly ... [the] dictates of anyone in authority over him, and who refuses to protest — even mildly — any unwarranted transgressions into his professional domain." In the early 1960s, the UFT's founders focused their efforts on angry young men in the junior high schools, and were completely surprised — and unaffected — when thousands of female elementary school teachers participated in early UFT actions. When, in the late 1960s, the UFT was locked in bitter conflict with Black community activists rather than with central administrators, union leaders would again view inflexibility as a virtue rather than a failing.[4]

The Teachers Union

Today's UFT traces its ideological and organizational roots to New York's Teachers Union, formed by Henry Linville and other social democrats. Through electoral campaigns and, especially, labor organization, social democrats sought to extend political democracy to economic life. Social democrats believed that the United States could evolve gradually toward socialism without a fundamental re-ordering of its political structure; that if distinctions of class could wither, other, more superficial social divisions would disappear even more easily; and that the U.S. might achieve a universally held culture, with universal standards of judgment, into which all would assimilate. Racial problems, in this view, were largely caused by and subservient to class conflicts. The social democratic response to American racism received its most famous expression from Eugene Debs, who defended "the Negro's right to work, live and develop his manhood, educate his children, and fulfill his destiny" equally with whites. Still, he claimed, "The Socialist Party is the Party of the whole working class, regardless of color," and therefore it had "nothing special to offer the Negro."[5]

Aspiring to professional respectability while espousing a mildly reformist vision of socialism, New York's social democratic teacher unionists placed more faith in discrete lobbying campaigns than in mass demonstrations. Until the 1930s, Linville and his followers retained firm command of the Teachers Union, but

JEAN-CLAUDE LEJEUNE

amid the growing activism and radicalism of the Depression years, teachers began to demand that the union take a more militant stand on school issues and broader political questions. When a Communist-led rank-and-file coalition won control of the Teachers Union in the 1935, the original Socialist leadership bolted the TU and formed the Teachers Guild, an organization which soon won the backing of the American Federation of Labor and in 1960 gave rise to the United Federation of Teachers .

Following the 1935 split, commitments to social justice animated both Teachers Union and Teachers Guild activities. But they were not always the same commitments. The Communist-led TU, notes historian Robert Iversen, attracted large numbers of teachers both through its "vision of a better world" and through its "indefatigable militancy and organizational skill in day-to-day struggle."[6] Despite the exodus of the social-democratic faction and the opposition of school officials to teacher unionism, the TU grew from 1,200 members in 1935 to 6,500 in 1938.[7]

One of the most significant differences between the TU's new leadership and Linville's more moderate group was its response to school racism, which the TU now made a major focus of its work. Although Blacks constituted only a small percentage of New York's students in the 1930s, school segregation and discrimination were already well-established. "Old, poorly equipped and overcrowded" schools were a primary

---

Teachers Union members joined with parents and community activists to organize pickets against the brutal corporal punishment of Black students and to secure the construction of Harlem's first new schools in decades.

---

source of Black discontent, a 1935 city investigation reported, and "many of the white teachers" assigned to Harlem schools "regard the appointment as a sort of punishment."[8] Even after he became disillusioned with Communism and left the Party, former Communist leader George Charney fondly recalled TU's militant activism:

> Pressing their demands for better schools, more schools, textbook revisions, Negro teachers and principals, free lunches, and so forth ... mothers came [to meetings] *en masse* to organize programs, assign delegations, and join in city-wide activities. In every school, white teachers, with the active support of the Teachers' Union, came forward to collaborate with the parents in this inspired effort to transform a community through education.[9]

Alice Citron, a leader in the overlapping Communist and Teachers Union circles of the 1930s, epitomized Depression-era anti-racist school organizing. In her Harlem classroom, Citron's lessons included original plays drawn from Black history, and she compiled bibliographies on Black life for other teachers. After the end of the school day, she volunteered in campaigns to institute a free lunch program, the celebration of Negro History Week, and improvement of school facilities.[10]

The theory on which TU based its anti-racist campaigning originated in the American Communist

Party. Extrapolating from the crucial role played by national minorities in the Russian Revolution, and influenced by demands for African-American self-determination, Communists reasoned that the union of the working class and Black community could catalyze the formation of a revolutionary movement capable of challenging American capitalism. Even if the Communist vision of self-determination for an "oppressed Negro nation" has rightly been dismissed as "a bit of 'fatuous romance,'" notes historian Mark Solomon, it led Communists "to deal with racial issues and attitudes in ways that were totally beyond the awareness and comprehension of most white Americans," and gave rise to "the most determined efforts of a predominantly white organization to achieve equality since the abolitionists."[11]

TU members joined with parents and community activists to organize pickets against the brutal corporal punishment of Black students and to secure the construction of Harlem's first new schools in decades. For almost twenty years, TU-led coalitions in Harlem and Brooklyn remained New York's most militant and effective grassroots school reform effort. Although most teachers never joined the TU's radical campaigns, once again, principled efforts improved working conditions and enriched teachers' work.

The TU's ability to simultaneously promote the interests of white teachers and of Black communities provided it no protection from the anti-Communist hysteria of the McCarthy era, when hundreds of activist teachers were forced out of the school system and parents were cowed into ending association with "subversives." In 1950, the Board of Education declared that neither it nor school supervisors and administrators was permitted to "negotiate, confer, or deal with or recognize [the Teachers Union] in relation to any grievances or any personal or professional problems, nor grant to said Teachers Union any of the rights or privileges accorded to any teacher organization." The ban, which lasted until 1962, destroyed the TU and cleared the way for the rise of the UFT.

The Teachers Guild and the UFT

Even in the heyday of the TU, Guild activists were promoting an alternative vision of teacher unionism, one that would lead directly to the establishment of the United Federation of Teachers and through it to the transformation of teacher organizing across the United States.

Within the Guild, a younger generation of teachers combined the mild reformism of Linville's generation with the militancy of their Communist competitors.

The Guild, according to veteran socialist and future UFT leader Jeannette DiLorenzo, "was a social movement as well as a trade union movement." Like many future UFT leaders, DiLorenzo had grown up in a home where "the religion" was "being part of an international movement." She studied socialism and Marxism at the Rand School and honed organizational and leadership skills in the Young People's Socialist League. Through countless meetings, debates, and bare-knuckled ideological and organizational battles, future UFT and AFT leaders mastered a vision of teacher unionism which they would maintain steadfastly through future decades. "I never stopped to analyze whether it was good people I was working for" DiLorenzo would remember. "It was the idea; it was working for a better world."[12]

When the Civil Right Movement arose in the South in the 1950s, the Guild's response was shaped by its continuing commitment to the Debsian ideal of full opportunity for workers of all races. Prodded by the Guild, as early as 1951, the AFT voted to charter no new locals that practiced racial discrimination, and by 1956 the union ordered southern affiliates to desegregate or be expelled. The AFT's efforts contrasted with those of the National Education Association, which did not fully desegregate until the 1970s.[13]

A vision of uniting all teachers and a strong commitment to unionism remained hallmarks of the New York AFT local when the Guild reconstituted itself as the UFT in 1960. "The goals of the embattled teachers," UFT founder Dave Selden claimed, "were the usual worker goals—higher wages, better benefits and improved working conditions. Perhaps the ultimate goals were higher status and dignity."[14] AFT President Carl Megel argued in 1962 against equating teachers with such professionals as doctors and lawyers: "A doctor or a lawyer is a businessman.... A teacher is a worker. You are a day laborer."[15]

When the UFT initiated its organizing campaign, it received tremendous support from the labor movement. Unions donated tens of thousands of dollars and lent field workers for the 1961 election in which the UFT won the right to represent New York's 43,000 teachers. Noting that white-collar employees had come to outnumber blue-collar workers in the United States, UFT Pres. Charles Cogen acclaimed the election as labor's biggest collective bargaining victory since the UAW organized Ford's River Rouge Plant in 1941.[16]

While portraying teachers as workers, UFT leaders also sought to promote teacher professionalism. If a teacher were "considered a production worker," UFT founder Dave Selden conceded, such issues as class size would be non-negotiable questions of educational policy rather than issues of working conditions. "But a teacher is not merely a production worker. He is a professional," and like other professionals, Selden argued, teachers had a right to be "self-directed and use their judgment in their work." By this definition, he argued, teachers might rightly negotiate over class-size not because large classes "sweated" teachers into undue hardship but because teachers rightly had a say in pedagogical issues.[17]

Unionists' understanding of teachers' work was not the only reason they invoked teacher professionalism as well as industrial unionism. The emergence of teacher unionism signaled important changes in American economic and political life. After World War II, automation and deindustrialization led to a decline in the number of number of factory jobs, and together with McCarthy-era repression and pro-management changes in labor law, to an even steeper drop in blue-collar unionism. Meanwhile, the number of state and local government jobs mushroomed. New York City alone lost 40% of its one million manufacturing jobs between 1950 and 1969, but increased its 375,000 government jobs by 40%.[18]

Union leaders were keenly aware of changes in the labor force, changes which made organizing groups such as teachers crucial to the future of the labor movement. When Brotherhood of Electrical Workers President James B. Carey addressed the NEA's 1962 convention, he pointed to the UFT's New York campaign as a model for teachers across the United States. The NEA's simple professionalism, Carey argued, "implies that your *craft* is somewhat above this world of ours; it implies a detachment, a remoteness from the daily battle of the streets, in the neighbor-

JEAN-CLAUDE LEJEUNE

hood, and in the cities." Without unions, he warned, teachers would lack decent wages and thus the ability to "afford integrity and honesty" in their work.[19] Another union official made the big picture plain. "How long will the file clerk go on thinking a union is below her dignity," he asked *Business Week*, "when the teacher next door belongs?"[20]

The synthesis of industrial unionism and professionalism proved immensely popular with teachers in New York and across the United States. Still, teachers' self-directed activity involves the direction of other persons. Inevitably, the new professionalism distanced city teachers from the urban communities in which they worked. Nowhere was the potential for conflict between urban teachers and the families they serve more clear than in New York.

By the late 1960s, the racial politics of education, together with wider changes in urban life, had undermined Black activists' faith in the good will of white teachers. The UFT never applied to local race-relations problems the militant commitment to racial equality

which informed its response to Southern struggles. Among the accomplishments of which the union boasted to teachers, for instance, was its having "killed the Superintendent's plan to force teachers to transfer to difficult schools."[21] In 1964, when over 400,000 of New York's one million students boycotted school in order to press for integration, the UFT declined to endorse the protest.[22]

Following the failure of the campaign to integrate New York's schools, Black activists increasingly demanded that school curricula and jobs be controlled by Blacks themselves. In 1968, experimental local school boards in Brooklyn's Ocean Hill-Brownsville neighborhood and the IS 201 district in Harlem became the focal points of New York's political life. After the Ocean Hill-Brownsville board attempted to remove 13 teachers from the district's schools, the UFT went out on strike for much of the fall of 1968. By the end of the year, the UFT had won its strikes and effectively ended the movement for decentralized "community control" of schooling.

In defense of the union's position, UFT leaders argued that the same principles of race-blind due process and interracial solidarity that had led them to support the Civil Rights Movement justified their opposition to community control. Nevertheless, in the context of the school conflict, invocations of professional autonomy increasingly dominated Debsian notions of working-class solidarity. Teachers, future AFT president Sandra Feldman claimed on the eve of the 1968 conflict, "in general support civil rights and equal educational opportunity, but their commitment to a fight for improved schools was .... largely, and understandably, self-interest ... a struggle to create a respected profession from a beleaguered, downgraded occupation."[23] "We don't deny their equality," a white teacher claimed while walking a UFT picket line, "but they shouldn't get it by pulling down others who have just come up. It's wrong and reactionary for them to pit their strength against a group that struggled for years to make teaching a profession."[24] "It has always been the intent of the UFT," Al Shanker claimed in the face of Black demands, "that community participation does not mean that those decisions under professional control should be surrendered." Union teachers, he stated bluntly, "will not continue to teach in any school or district where professional decisions are made by laymen."[25]

In addition to the heightened passions of the moment, the very conditions of urban school teaching contributed to teachers' willingness to distance themselves from the communities in which they worked. By the late 1960s, a majority of New York's students were Black or Latino; meanwhile, most teachers were white. An increasingly wide physical, cultural, and political gulf separated teachers, who could abandon cities for suburban retreats, from their students, who lived in decaying urban neighborhoods. The majority of teachers, New York teacher activist and future urban school reformer Deborah Meier has observed, brought prejudices against poor minority children to their work, and "rather than undermining these prejudices," the teaching experience "arouses them."[26] Amid the troubling and visible tragedy of widespread minority student failure, adherence to seemingly uniform, race-blind standards of instruction asserted teachers' professionalism while absolving them of responsibility for their ineffectiveness.

The same economic changes that led the labor movement to organize teachers and other white-collar workers also undermined the UFT's invocations of working-class inter-racial solidarity as a vehicle for advancing Black freedom. As factories disappeared, industrial democracy could no longer animate the imagination of New York's poor. Their grievances — welfare rules, police brutality, poor city services, urban renewal, and school policies — were the results of an oppressive state rather than an oppressive boss. Indeed, as Black teacher activist Rhody McCoy argued, the people of Ocean Hill-Brownsville were a "community" because "they were involved in struggles with poverty programs, with political machines .... They've had common goals and interests."[27] At a time when community activists in New York and across the United States increasingly embraced demands for Black Power, the April 1968 assassination of Martin Luther King, Jr. dashed any residual faith in the promise of racial integration.

Despite the changes in urban life, UFT leaders insisted throughout the 1968 conflict that the social democratic politics of interracial solidarity remained the surest means of securing real power for Black Americans. Current AFT president Sandra Feldman was a leader in the UFT's 1968 struggle. Community control, she argued, "strengthens segregation and places upon poor communities the burden of creating desperately needed, massive, substantive, program-matic changes in their schools." Only the federal government, Feldman insisted, "can provide the kind of resources needed" to substantially improve inner city education "and only a massive coalition of forces can prod Congress into action."[28]

By 1968, however, U.S. government commitment to social welfare programs and racial equity had already begun to ebb. When AFL-CIO leaders endorsed the UFT's 1968 fight against community control, how-ever, it was because of the union's importance "not only for the future of teacher unionism but for the growth and expansion of white collar and public service employee unions as well." Even as they en-dorsed the UFT, labor leaders signaled the degree to which teacher unionism had distanced itself from the needs of working-class communities.[29]

The 1968 school crisis established the UFT's powerful role in school politics and urban life, a role that benefited teachers in later salary renegotiations. Moreover, the same ideals of professional autonomy that brought the UFT into vicious conflict with Black community activists led it to be an early advocate of gay teachers' right to be judged by their work alone and not their identity.[30]

Victory in 1968 was, however, expensive for New York's teachers. In the years following the school conflict, racial tensions demoralized school work and undermined the very liberal coalition that the union claimed to seek. In an earlier time, the UFT's rhetoric of equal opportunity, due process, industrial unionism, and professionalism might have enabled members to transcend narrower views and individual bigotry. In 1968, the UFT's anachronistic invocation of interracial working-class solidarity legitimized racial inequality in the contested world of the schools, a result that has led virtually every commentator to conclude that "no crisis in recent New York City labor relations history evokes such despair as events ... in 1968."[31]

The Past and Future of Social Justice Unionism

Self-interest alone is inadequate as a guide to personal action or social analysis in part because self-interest is never really clear. "Conditions," John Dewey observes, are not "fixed or even reasonably stable .... Social conditions are running in different, often opposed directions. Because of this fact the educator ... is constantly compelled to make a choice. With what phase and direction of social forces will he throw in his energies?"[32] Teachers' notions of self-interest — and the alliances to which they give rise — inevitably reflect the theories and beliefs which shape their interpretations of social reality.

Teacher unions have at times challenged the inequalities of American life, and fostered broader demands for the public good. At other moments, they have placed teachers' immediate interests and privileges of teachers above more expansive ideals. And often, teachers have been served reasonably well by such visions, even if their more disadvantaged students have not been. But whatever their short-term appeal, teachers are also harmed by theories which lead them to ally themselves with class, gender, and racial privilege. In order to protect self-interest, public school teachers must, in the long run, protect the public interest.

However much they have differed, the men and women who shaped New York's teacher unionism — people such as Henry Linville, Alice Citron, Al Shanker — have been animated by expansive social visions. This should not be surprising. Although today's attacks on public schools — vouchers, privatization, and the like — are in many ways new, public schooling has always been threatened by those who put privilege above the common good. Will today's attacks on schools and other public services lead teacher unionists to imagine ideologies responsive to today's realities? Will unionists find means of convincing fellow teachers that threatening circumstances demand new coalitions and not circle-the-wagons reaction? The history of teacher unionism raises questions that only its future will answer. **TTU**

DAN PERLSTEIN IS A HISTORIAN WHOSE WORK FOCUSES ON AMERICAN EDUCATION. HE TEACHES IN THE UNIVERSITY OF CALIFORNIA AT BERKELEY'S GRADUATE SCHOOL OF EDUCATION.

Footnotes

[1] Marjorie Murphy, *Blackboard Unions: The AFT and the NEA, 1900-1980* (Ithaca: Cornell University Press, 1990), p. 23.

[2] United Federation of Teachers, "Class Struggles: The UFT Story," www.uft.org/about/hist1.html.

[3] David Tyack, *The One Best System: A History of American Urban Education* (Cambridge: Harvard University Press, 1974), p. 267.

[4] Charles Cogen, "The President's Column," *United Teacher*, May 1960, p. 2; Charles Cogen, "The Teacher's Public Image," *United Teacher*, June 1963, p. 3.

[5] Debs quoted in Jervis Anderson, *A. Philip Randolph: A Biographical Portrait* (New York: Harcourt Brace Jovanovich, 1973), pp. 148-9.

[6] Robert Iversen, *The Communists & The Schools* (New York: Harcourt, Brace and Co., 1959), p. 194.

[7] Ruth Jacknow Markowitz, *My Daughter, the Teacher: Jewish Teachers in the New York City Schools* (New Brunswick: Rutgers University Press, 1993), pp. 154, 158, 169.

[8] Quoted in Celia Lewis Zitron, *The New York City Teachers Union, 1916-1964: A Story of Educational and Social Commitment* (New York: Humanities Press, 1969), pp. 86-7.

[9] George Charney, *A Long Journey* (Chicago: Quadrangle Books, 1968), p. 99.

[10] Alice Citron interview, 6 Jan. 1981, Oral History of the American Left Collection, Tamiment Institute Library, New York University; Mark Naison, *Communists in Harlem During the Depression* (Urbana: University of Illinois Press, 1983), p. 216.

[11] Mark Solomon, *Red and Black: Communism and Afro-Americans, 1929-1935* (New York: Garland, 1988), pp. 106, 163.

[12] Jeannette DiLorenzo, interview, UFT Oral History Collection, United Federation of Teachers Papers, Robert F. Wagner Labor Archives, New York University (hereafter UFT Papers).

[13] Rolland Dewing, "Teacher Organizations and Desegregation," *Phi Delta Kappan*, Jan. 1968, pp. 257-60.

[14] David Selden, *The Teacher Rebellion* (Washington: Howard University Press, 1985), pp. 47-8, 68, 109.

[15] T. M. Stinnett, *Turmoil in Teaching: A History of the Organizational Struggle for America's Teachers* (New York: Macmillan, 1968), p. 159.

[16] Charles Cogen, "President's Column," *United Teacher*, Dec. 1963, p. 4.

[17] David Selden, "Class Size and the New York Contract," *Phi Delta Kappan*, Mar. 1964, pp. 283-87; Selden, *The Teacher Rebellion*, p. 82.

[18] Benjamin Klebaner, ed., *New York City's Changing Economic Base* (New York: Pica Press, 1981), pp. 2, 128. *Employment & Earnings: States & Areas, 1939-1978* (Washington, DC: United States Department of Labor, Bureau of Labor Statistics, 1979), p. 423.

[19] James Carey, "Address," *Addresses and Proceedings* (Washington, DC: National Education Association, 1962), pp. 48-49.

[20] *Business Week*, 30 Dec. 1961, quoted in Stinnett, *Turmoil in Teaching*, p. 56.

[21] "UFT's Record of Gains for Teachers," *United Teacher*, June 1962, p. 4.

[22] "Executive board minutes," *United Teacher*, 24 Jan. 1964, p. 7; Richard Montague and Alfred Hendricks, "The Battle for the Schools," *New York Post*, 2 Feb. 1964, p. 22.

[23] Sandra Feldman, "The Growth of Teacher Consciousness: 1967" (New York: League for Industrial Democracy, no date), p. 4.

[24] Bill Kovach, "Racist and Anti-Semitic Charges Strain Old Negro-Jewish Ties," *New York Times*, 23 Oct. 1968, p. 1.

[25] Albert Shanker, "UFT Statement on Decentralization" (fall 1968), p. 5, Box 1, folder 1, Teachers Action Caucus Papers, Tamiment Institute.

[26] Deborah Meier, interview, New York City, 11 Sept. 1990.

[27] McCoy, interview, in *Why Teachers Strike: Teachers' Rights and Community Control*, Melvin Urofsky, ed. (Garden City, NY: Doubleday, 1970), p. 118.

[28] Sandra Feldman, "N.Y. City Decentralization," *New America*, 31 Mar. 1968, p. 5; Sandra Feldman, "N.Y. City Decentralization" (Part II), *New America*, 15 Apr. 1968, p. 6.

[29] "AFL-CIO Leaders Back Teacher Union," *New York Times*, 17 Sept. 1968, p. 41.

[30] AFT Executive Council, motion, 1970, www.aft.org/humanrights/issues.htm.

[31] Mark Maier, *City Unions: Managing Discontent in New York City* (New Brunswick, NJ: Rutgers University Press, 1987), 127.

[32] John Dewey, "Can Education Share in Social Reconstruction?" *The Social Frontier* 1 (Oct. 1934), p. 12.

Facing Tough Decisions

BY HERBERT KOHL

Since the turn of the century, New York City has been in the national forefront of teacher unionism. Educational author Herbert Kohl taught in New York City public schools in the 1960s. Below, he reflects on some of the controversies of that time, controversies that still confront teachers today. For a broader look at the history of teacher unionism in New York City, see Dan Perlstein's, "If Not Now, When?" on p. 86.

JUST BEFORE MY GRANDFATHER DIED HE GAVE ME SOME advice. "Herbert," he said, "when you go out on strike carry your picket sign on a two-by-four." For those naive in the ways of early union struggles, the advice he was giving me was to fight the bosses, the police, and anyone else who would interfere with the struggles of working people. It was an earlier version of Malcolm X's maxim: "By any means necessary." Pop had taken the pledge and he was a union man as much as he was a father and grandfather. Crossing a picket line was, to him, a sin — one worth fighting over.

When I became an elementary school teacher, there was no doubt in my mind about joining the United Federation of Teachers. That was 1961, and I was a student at Teachers College, Columbia University. It was the time when a vote for the bargaining agent for the New York City teachers was being held. As prospective teachers, we were asked to cast a mock vote. The faculty at TC made it clear that their preference was National Education Association affiliation. We students voted overwhelmingly for the United Federation of Teachers (UFT). The gap between our professors' desires and our understanding of the need for a union, not just a professional organization, was indicative of the distance between Teachers College's staff and their students.

My first teaching job in 1962 was at PS 145 on Manhattan's West Side. Naturally I joined the union

— the UFT, which was the only choice we had. There were five of us in the chapter and I became the alternate delegate at the school by default. Ironically I didn't know anything about teaching, had hardly begun my career, and yet was central to our union chapter. What I didn't know at the time was that there was another, older union represented at the school, the Teachers Union (TU), Local 5 of the American Federation of Teachers, which was in the process of

JANET BROWN MCCRACKEN

disbanding. It had two members at the school, both on the verge of retirement.

TU was founded in 1916 by a group of radical New York City school teachers. On March 10, 1916, they affiliated with the American Federation of Labor and in 1941, were expelled from the American Federation of Teachers for refusing to take an oath that no members were communists or subversives. They were replaced in the AFT by Local 2, the United Federation of Teachers, which by the time I entered the world of teacher unions was the dominant teacher organization in New York City.

Nevertheless, I was in the UFT, which itself was looked on as a radical cabal at the school. Most teachers would have nothing to do with the union and thought we were troublemakers. That year the UFT called one of the first teachers' strikes in U.S. history.

However, the two older teachers who were members of TU until its last days taught me a lot about teaching and about what a teachers union might be. They reflected their union's view that a teachers organization had educational responsibilities, had to be accountable to the community it served, and had to be militant in the service of the children and to issues of justice and equity. In addition, it had to develop curriculum and take stands on pedagogical, race, and gender issues. It was not to merely become a vehicle for increased wages and a protector of teachers from the communities they served. These viewpoints were reflected in the types of panels they had at their Annual Educational Conferences: "'Every Child's Right to Knowledge," "Freeing the Capacity of Every Child to Learn." and "The Best Possible Education — for the Few or for All?" [1]

In fact, the two members of TU at PS 145 were the only teachers who helped me. They gave me books for my students and hints about how to teach reading. Most important, they provided a sense that teaching for justice and equity could indeed be at the center of one's work without being dogmatic or authoritarian.

A Successful Strike

Nevertheless, I was in the UFT, which itself was looked on as a radical cabal at the school. Most teachers would have nothing to do with the union and thought we were troublemakers. That year the UFT called one of the first teachers' strikes in U.S. history.

At that time it was illegal for public employees to strike, and the union leadership, led by Charles Cogen, was opposed to the strike. However, the strike vote was carried in the delegate assembly by a small majority of teachers, most of whom worked in the junior high and high school divisions.

I remember being out on the picket line on the first day of that successful strike. The principal of the school was out with coffee for us and even brought bagels and cream cheese. He wanted the strike to succeed, not for union reasons but out of sheer self-interest. Anticipating the possibility of a successful strike, the administrators association in New York had succeeded in getting the state legislature to pass a bill guaranteeing to the administrators proportional salary raises in any strike settlement. As a result of the strike, my wages went from $5,200 a year to $6,200 a year, a $1,000 increase. However, his salary, which exceeded $25,000, increased by at least $2,500. Despite our victory, the gap between teachers' and administrators' wages widened.

The nicest thing that happened to us young teachers on the picket line was that Bayard Rustin, who lived in the neighborhood, came by and told stories of his union experiences. I remember being proud to be part of the struggle for equity, justice, and teachers' rights, to be honored by Rustin, and to honor my own grandfather.

One major result of the strike was dues check-off. Our small chapter of five members grew overnight to include almost all of the 45 teachers at the school. During the first meeting of the newly constituted chapter, new officers were chosen, eliminating us "radicals" and putting the chapter, as one teacher said, "on a more even keel."

The next school year, I was transferred to another school in East Harlem and remained in the union, though I was one of a few dissonant voices in a conservative chapter. The only issues the newly constituted union seemed concerned with were working conditions and salary. When some of us brought up issues of curriculum, faculty racism, low expectations, and even physical and verbal abuse of students, we were silenced. At that point I became alienated from the union.

Several years later, the conflict between teachers' self-interest and the demands of parents and community activists exploded. Community leaders called for greater teacher accountability, more resources for schools, and eventually community control of schools. The initial focus of the conflict was the opening of the newly constructed Intermediate School 201 on 128th

Street and Madison Avenue. The Board of Education originally promised to make 201 an integrated school but abandoned that idea, just as it abandoned all bussing and desegregation plans for the entire city. This was 1964 during the height of the Civil Rights Movement. The Black Power movement was emerging and the Young Lords were organizing in the Puerto Rican community. With the refusal of officials to integrate the schools, parents and community activists abandoned the idea of desegregated schools and decided that the only way to create quality education was to have community control of schools — something which had always been the case in white affluent communities.

An Agonizing Decision

By this time Albert Shanker was head of the United Federation of Teachers. As the controversy at Intermediate School (IS) 201 erupted, the community actually took control of the school and staffed it with a variety of educators, activists, artists, and other community members who had skills and cared about children. The community demanded an African-American administrator, community accountability, and respect for the children and the parents. The UFT, under Shanker's leadership, set up picket lines around the school to prevent students and parents from coming in.

To me this was one of the greatest ironies I have encountered in education: teachers striking a school, trying to prevent children from entering the building, and keeping parents at bay. I saw it as an expression of scorn for the community and disrespect for the children's ability, tinged with racism. I had to take a stand for or against the parents and the community. I decided to cross the teachers' picket line.

Crossing the picket line was difficult — I worried about what my grandfather would think, remembering his union pledge and the unquestioned loyalty every working person was supposed to feel for unions. But, weighing the lives of the children and the attempt by the union to protect incompetence, I chose the parents and the children. This was one of the most agonizing decisions I have ever had to make and, though I would do it again if faced with the choice, I still worry about it making the spirit of my grandfather restless and angry.

If I was clear about anything after my first six years of being a teacher and an educational activist, it was that the first priority had to be the children. Loyalty to any idea, institution, or organization, was secondary. If the children are nurtured and are treated with dignity and affection, if their voices are honored and their

thoughts respected, if their culture and language are welcomed, and if they are acquiring skills and learning about the world and themselves, then I am willing to be loyal to the learning community and the union that represents it. But if humiliation and incompetence characterize an institution, then I oppose it and am willing to take the consequences of speaking out against it.

This controversy predated Ocean Hill-Brownsville, but the community people and educators involved in IS 201 and Ocean Hill-Brownsville knew each other and later became allies in struggle. My taking sides with the parents and community at IS 201 made me enemies within the teachers union, including teachers I had worked with. I was not the only teacher who crossed the line, however. I know that to this day, rancor exists between New York City teachers who supported the community activists and those who supported the union leadership. It is, in my mind, time to get beyond this. But questions of deep loyalty and questions of racism and support for children and communities are still at the heart of the conflicts that currently challenge all public educators.

Reconnecting to the Union

I reconnected with the union in Berkeley, California, during the 1970s. At the time I was running an alternative public high school, called Other Ways, which was on the margins of the system. We had funding from the Carnegie Corporation of New York and some extra money from small foundations. We also managed to get a contract with the school system which allowed us to develop our own curriculum, hire whomever we wanted, and develop our own procedures for evaluation.

The Berkeley Federation of Teachers allowed me to become an honorary member. None of us knew what that meant other than that it was clear that our charter-like school was not in conflict with the other good schools in Berkeley. We were meeting needs not being met by the system itself. It was a friendly standoff, a marriage of convenience which we, at Other Ways, really appreciated. What we tried to work out informally was a way to support teacher unions and educational innovation at the same time.

The arrangement only lasted for a few years before our school and a number of other Berkeley alternative high schools were eliminated as the district became more conservative educationally. But what was important was that members of the Berkeley Federation of Teachers were willing to sit down and talk education, and begin to conceptualize what a progressive and open teachers' union might look like. It is a pleasure these days to have the opportunity to speak to people in union groups like TURN who are embarking on similar projects.

That is our challenge now. I have had many more complex exchanges with teachers organizations since the 1970s as I've continued to teach on the margins of the public schools. However I see the role of the unions (both NEA and AFT) shifting towards the defensive these days. Years of forgetting children and community, and of neglecting pedagogical issues and turning them over to academic professionals or outside consultants, have rusted the minds of too many school-based people.

One way to keep the unions strong is to take back education. Taking back education does not merely mean fending off vouchers, resisting or trying to control charter schools, and complaining about privatization. It has, from my perspective, to do fundamentally with educators in the public schools showing that they know what they are doing, that they think about learning as much as they think about salaries and security, and perhaps more than anything, that they are on the side of the children they teach and the communities they serve. If the unions cannot mobilize themselves for this, I see a long, slow process of attrition and death of the dream of public education providing equity, opportunity, and quality learning for all children.

As Rose Russell, one of the central figures in the old Teachers Union said at its last formal meeting in 1964:

> The fight must go on in new ways — some easier, some harder ... I believe there must be a complete overhaul of those false educational values based on a frantic race for grades, with super-specialized, speed-up training for a dehumanized elite, and a dead end for the majority of our children.

> I believe that teachers must be well-prepared, well-paid, well-intentioned towards their pupils, and free from the pressures of small minds, from whatever quarter they may come.

> I believe the world of tomorrow will be, because it must be, a world of equal opportunity for all.

> This is a tall order. We teachers can play a small but significant part. Above all we must, we must ourselves believe in this, and teach our children of all races and colors to respect each other, to live together, learn together, play together, and enrich each other's lives thereby.

> But this world of tomorrow demands first of all that there be a world today. So you see, there is a lot to be done.

> Wherever you are, you will find the ways to help, and so will I, you may be sure. Our paths are bound to cross many times, for our training in the [Teachers] Union, and the bonds of friendship and kinship it created and nourished, will be everlastingly with us.[2] **TTU**

HERBERT KOHL IS AN EDUCATOR AND WRITER WHOSE MOST RECENT BOOKS ARE *THE DISCIPLINE OF HOPE* (SIMON & SCHUSTER, 1998) AND *A GRAIN OF POETRY* (HARPER COLLINS, 1999).

Footnotes

[1] Celia Lewis Zitron, *The New York City Teachers Union 1916-1964: A Story of Educational and Social Commitment* (New York: Humanities Press, 1968), p. 77.
[2] Ibid., p. 261.

Prospects for a
United Teachers Union

What Happened to the NEA/AFT Merger?

BY ANN BASTIAN

ONE OF THE BIGGEST MARRIAGES IN MODERN politics almost took place the summer of 1998: the merger of the National Education Association (NEA) and the American Federation of Teachers (AFT). But when the NEA delegates met in New Orleans in June, they rejected the prenuptial agreement and recommended a longer and more cautious engagement.

The prospect of merger was tantalizing, in part because the scale was so impressive and the logic of unity so compelling. Here would have been a union of 3.3 million members, over 2.3 million from the NEA and over 950,000 from AFT. Collectively, the two unions represent 85% of all public school teachers, the most highly unionized sector of the workforce. Members are based in primary and secondary schools in every community — urban, suburban, and rural — and operate the second largest sector of the economy, generating $348 billion annually, right behind the health-care industry.

Public education is also at the heart of contemporary social politics.

Schooling is not only the oldest and largest government entitlement program. It is also the bedrock institution of the public sector, embodying core ideals of opportunity and our collective responsibility for social needs. While it has long been contested whether the dominant needs that public schools serve are corporate or democratic, utilitarian or civic, the concept of the public school as a necessary community institution has not been at risk for most of this century.

But the concept and the institution are at risk today, in at least three arenas. First, public education is under unrelenting political assault from the Right and its privatization agenda. Nothing has better unified entrepreneurial, libertarian, and religious conservatives than their quest for a market-based education system through school vouchers and the repeal of educational entitlements for children of color.

Second, there is an ongoing crisis in urban education. Social neglect and government retrenchment have combined with a dramatic polarization of wealth over the past two decades to structurally erode urban districts, placing nearly 40% of inner-city children at risk of school failure.

Third, too many schools, across all states and districts, have not evolved past the factory model of the last century to become learning organizations in the information age. Even for decent school systems, the status quo in the face of rising expectations has produced a decline in public confidence and willingness to invest in public education, at a time when only one in four households has children at school.

The prospective NEA-AFT merger was put forth as a vehicle for teachers to take initiative in addressing these challenges, particularly the threat from the Right. For its proponents, the merger promised to reconcile a bitter rivalry, break down each union's insularity, and shift the focus outward. The consolidation of political capital would have been especially formidable — the new union would have exceeded the Christian Coalition by two million members.

More Time Needed?

For all of its promise, the merger failed overwhelmingly in the hands of NEA delegates. Only 42% supported the proposal, far short of the 67% required for ratification. Did the partners suffer irreconcilable differences? Or did they just need more time?

Reports on the vote focused on what delegates perceived as critical differences between the two unions. Some felt the merger threatened NEA's democratic representative assembly process; some were threatened by AFT's history of militant strikes, and others by the fear that AFL-CIO affiliation would degrade their professionalism.

What is striking is not just that opposition spanned a wide spectrum of political consciousness, from concerns about union democracy to class snobbery. It is also striking that so many of the reasons cited were superficial and misperceived. The reality is that the two teacher unions are not profoundly different.

To be sure, the NEA and AFT have traveled different paths. The NEA is a century old and most of that time has been spent as a professional association and advocacy organization. The AFT was forged as a union in the public employee recognition struggles of the 1960s.

NEA is a sprawling network of powerful and autonomous state associations, run by a permanent cadre of staff (sometimes labeled bureaucratic), with its largest base in suburban districts. The AFT has had, until recently, one leader (sometimes labeled auto-cratic) presiding over a chain of centralized locals in the big industrial cities. The NEA has stood outside the rest of the labor movement and has, by and large, espoused the most consistently progressive social platform of any union. The AFT has been in the thick of AFL-CIO politics, on the side of Cold Warriors as well as social liberals. The two unions also have different organizational cultures. Stylistically, the AFT is from Mars, the NEA is from Venus.

But in their core constructions, both the NEA and AFT are quite similar. Both are large, relatively strong trade unions and have been for 30 years. Their power has been built around collective bargaining muscle, legislative brokering, and the scale of their memberships. Both have mounted militant strikes, both have strong and weak locals, both have progressive and reactionary forces, both have hierarchic and democratic practices. While AFT represents the old-line cities, NEA represents at least half the large and new cities, and its suburban districts now have funding crises just like the cities.

Both NEA and AFT locals are typically reactive to the school systems they operate within, and both tend to reflect the strengths and pathologies of those systems. Both have achieved substantial bread-and-butter gains for teachers, both have defended public education, both have neglected the communities that schools belong to.

Over the last decade, as the ground has shifted profoundly in education politics, the paths of the unions have converged even further. Both are being challenged to engage in education reform as a matter of survival for their membership and for public education itself. The national leaders of both unions have concluded that the era of adversarial collective bargaining and special-interest clout has left them isolated and vulnerable in this new era, which requires rebuilding school communities and broad political coalitions.

So both NEA and AFT leaders have recast their unions as reform agents. NEA President Bob Chase calls it "The New Unionism," stressing professional

A plenary session at the 1998 NEA convention.

issues of teacher empowerment that go beyond traditional employee rights. Generally consistent with the positions of AFT President Sandra Feldman, Chase's new unionism strives to get past the era of centralized and adversarial collective bargaining and move toward a "quality of work life" or co-management role within the local school and an active voice in retooling the profession.

If the differences are not particularly current or fundamental, did the merger fail tactically, because it wasn't adequately sold to the membership? Was the problem that NEA delegates wanted to go forward but couldn't shake old perceptions of the AFT? This interpretation is reinforced by the fact that the day after rejecting the merger proposal, NEA delegates reaffirmed their commitment to the concept of unity and authorized a new round of merger discussions.

However, there seems to be a deeper lesson here, captured precisely by the delegates' ambivalence:

Did the partners suffer irreconcilable differences? Or did they just need more time?

NEA wasn't ready for the merger because there is not yet a solid center in the union that accepts or understands the new paradigm in education politics and is ready to face the multiple challenges implied.

Merger is just one challenge, and perhaps the most technical. The overall challenge is to embrace a much enlarged mission of educational entitlement for children as well as professional empowerment for teachers. Without this new paradigm, there is no assurance that if or when the merger goes forward, it will produce the positive outcomes intended.

What Next?

The challenge of a new mission impacts the AFT just as forcefully as it does the NEA. The AFT delegates, meeting a month after the NEA, overwhelmingly ratified the principles of unity. But they too had mixed motives. Some AFT locals represent a broader mission for teacher unions, others are fixed in the power politics of a bygone era, some are simply looking for tactical allies in the midst of a siege.

To better picture the forces shaping both unions — and their potential merger — we can imagine multiple scenarios. One scenario flows from the progressives in both unions who embrace both union reform and school restructuring. A second could be directed by the old guard in each union who want to keep their fiefdoms intact. And a third could be built around the center forces in each union which have focused on

teacher professionalism.

Where are the "new unionists" in this? They range from progressive to centrist, depending on the balance they strike between the issues of equity and professionalism.

Scenario #1: Progressive Hopes

Many progressives saw the merger as a historic opportunity to reorient the unions internally as well as externally, locally as well as nationally. In a progressive scenario, the institutional change process would give activists a catalytic role. The new union would continue as a major line of defense against the Right's agenda, but it would also cultivate a growing awareness that organizing and coalition-building within communities is essential to sustain public schools educationally as well as politically.

A progressive version of the new union would link teacher interests in the decaying urban systems, the core of AFT, to the concerns of teachers in the suburban systems that dominate NEA. Teaching conditions would be more strongly identified with learning conditions for children, putting equity and social justice issues more clearly at the center of the union's agenda. The merger would provide openings for school reformers in both unions to push school restructuring — local school decision-making, professional development, peer review, community linkages, attention to learning styles, child-centered instruction, multiple approaches to assessment and accountability — efforts that would rebuild public credibility, collaboration, and investment.

Who are these progressives? In both unions, they are an amalgam of teacher activists who have focused on union reform and those who have focused on school reform. The two strands have increasingly overlapped, particularly in besieged urban systems.

They find their most coherent expression in the Teacher Union Reform Network (TURN), a discussion group of union leaders from 21 locals in the NEA and AFT. Drawn largely from major urban districts, TURN leaders represent some of the strongest models for unions helping teachers and their schools become more pro-active, professional, accountable, and responsive. These leaders also share an implicit equity perspective that school reform must address the alarming condition of urban schools and serve those most at risk (see article, p. 22).

Progressive viewpoints with a forceful focus on

equity are articulated through the journal *Rethinking Schools* and the union caucus in the National Coalition of Education Activists (NCEA). The latter group convened 30 leaders from both unions to issue a draft platform, "Social Justice Unionism," that clearly expresses the identity crisis facing the NEA and AFT (see pp. xx). While many progressive teachers also march under the banner of "new unionism," they worry that the emphasis on professionalism has tended to marginalize social equity issues.

Some NEA progressives opposed the merger on the grounds that the new structures were less formally democratic and the decision-making more centralized. But most seemed disappointed by the merger vote. Whether a new merger plan goes forward or not, progressives in the NEA and AFT are left with a series

---

Teacher unions can only succeed by linking the future of the teaching profession with the future of all the nation's children.

---

of challenges:

• How to forcefully safeguard employee rights and teacher gains while being a partner in building new school communities. There is a delicate balance in being an advocate but not adversarial, and being collaborative but not co-opted. The NEA and AFT locals best able to play leadership roles in reform efforts have been strong and well-led unions with solid collective-bargaining histories, that are also not locked into their collective-bargaining identities.

• How to address the gap between teacher interests as employees seeking higher reward and professionals seeking autonomy, and larger issues of accountability and equity that would improve learning conditions for all children. That gap is glaring in underfunded or restructuring school systems, where real trade-offs are demanded. Many teachers and their unions have been reluctant to broaden the bargaining table at those moments.

• How to bridge the two sets of concerns with social justice activism as well as vision. This task requires organizing strategies for moving the majority of union members beyond their immediate career or classroom concerns to an investment in the success of the system as a whole.

• How to increase the number of districts and schools with union involvement in school restructuring. There is a respectable roster of models, but not a

critical mass. The danger is that collaborative reform efforts will remain isolated as showcase schools and districts, without shifting the overall balance of educational or union practice. Progressive reformers need to be in the thick of union politics, regardless of merger prospects, if the center is to move in a new direction.

• How to play active and integrative roles on many fronts at once: internal union politics, external social politics, systemic and local school reform, peer organizing, instructional innovation, and, for many, day-to-day jobs in the classroom as well.

• How, on a local union level, to cultivate member participation, broaden union democracy, develop new leadership in teacher ranks, and expand the support network for activists. It seems especially important that strong locals develop organizational cultures that sustain more women and people of color in leadership, better reflecting both the teaching corps and urban communities.

Scenario #2: Restoration Politics

Progressives do not operate in a vacuum. There are significant old-guard forces in both unions, resisting a new paradigm for education politics and a new union mission. They are found in some of the AFT's big-city locals, with their highly centralized leadership structures, and in a fair number of the larger NEA state associations, run by presiding bureaucrats. They are clinging to the tradition of craft unionism, whether militant or utterly co-opted, which still exerts a powerful pull on the labor movement.

The old guard represent the prior power base of both unions, forged in the era of union recognition and expanding education budgets. For years, they have relied on rich coffers, hardball lobbying, campaign donations, and narrow agendas to pursue their interests in the statehouses, where they used to dominate the "education establishment" of administrators, elected officials, contractors, and support personnel. They built expedient coalitions at the leadership level around single issues, and only appealed to the public at the district level during contract disputes or votes on parcel taxes, levies, and bond issues. Their response to the call for teacher unionists to engage in educational improvement: "Children don't vote."

The old guard have also functioned with high levels of autonomy from the national offices, which nonetheless rely on them for firepower in the states. They can be equally distant from their membership, which is generally passive and often equally parochial. They embrace a narrow "them or us" mentality, that ironically may coincide with spirited union action against enemy school boards, administrators, or parents. "Them or us" coincides powerfully as well with the siege mentality of many teachers who find themselves isolated in classrooms, outsiders to their students' communities, and/or devalued as frontline professionals.

Within the NEA, the anti-merger charge was led by several state delegations dominated by old-guard forces seeking to retain their internal power. There is another sticking point: the AFT cities. The NEA old guard may well be concerned about the hefty voting blocs that large urban locals might bring to a merged state union from cities like New York, Chicago, Newark, or Detroit.

The old guard and much of their member base also seemed concerned about acquiring some responsibility for dealing with the educational failures of the old urban systems. Several reports from NEA's convention confirm a reactionary fear among some delegates that inclusion of the AFT cities will weaken their separate defense of suburban public education. It is a version of the "them or us" worldview, with troubling segregationist undertones around race and class.

The old guard and their base may prefer the status quo of separate unions. But one shouldn't underestimate their ability to influence a merger if their autonomy is secured under new terms. Nor should one underestimate their ability to dominate a new union, especially if the center is weak.

Then one can imagine a worst-case scenario. The merger would consolidate the stonewalling postures of the old guard toward reform. Or it might consume both unions in petty power politics inside the new institution — a process akin to wrangling over who will play first fiddle as Rome burns.

The primacy of warlord politics would likely set the union agenda at the lowest common denominator, meaning narrow teacher self-interest around pay, tenure, professional credentials, and veto power in the school change process. It would signal a retreat to parochialism and hand the high ground of reform to the numerically smaller, but far more strategic, activists of the Republican Right.

Pro-unity delegates demonstrate at the NEA convention in 1998 in New Orleans.

Scenario #3: Does the Center Hold?

The center, and probably the majority force, within each union appears to be a patchwork of tactical and strategic allies, drawn from both the "new unionists" and the old guard.

Although the "new unionism" camp has been bold in recognizing the new paradigm and seeking merger, it is cautious in staking out ground around school restructuring, the centrality of equity issues, and grassroots alliances with school communities. The more pragmatic and astute members of the old guard connect with the new unionists in recognizing that there has been a climate shift. Believing the best defense is offense, the pragmatists are willing to combine forces to project an image of teacher collaboration and improving schools. If this alliance prevails, it seems we would get the middle-ground scenario: the unions, merged or merely parallel, would continue along current trajectories.

The unifying agenda of this emerging center is actually "the new professionalism." Its attraction is that professional status issues allow union leaders to appeal to members' self-interest and career aspirations, while offering more to the public by way of national standards and accountability, and offering administrators and politicians the prospect of collaboration. The professional standards agenda gives the unions a central focus that can be simultaneously linked to reform and membership demands.

But in several key respects, this seems too narrow an agenda to meet either the external challenges facing education or the harsh realities facing many classroom teachers. The professionalism agenda has many of the elements of sophisticated craft unionism, including the concept of teachers as licensed contractors, with too few elements of social unionism, including how to change learning conditions for kids.

How will professional empowerment take place in classrooms of 40 children speaking 10 different languages? Will the career ladder reach high enough to fix the leaking roof in the computer lab? Will team teaching restore the after-school sports program or in-school family services? Will national accreditation create time for parent consultations or teach teachers how to talk with the community?

The professionalism agenda is not matched by an agenda for reconstructing urban schools, revising state funding formulas, integrating the increasingly white teaching corps, restoring affirmative action and language rights, combating the trend toward test-driven teaching, resisting the trend toward tracking and "creaming," and so much more. Most crucially, it does not include a commitment for standing together with local communities, across some difficult race and class divides, to oppose the Right's assault on all public entitlements, that have shredded the safety net for children, and put education on the chopping block as well.

The professionalism agenda is necessary but not sufficient. It embodies a conception of unionism that rests centrally on the self-interest of teachers, rather than on their mutual interests with children and their communities. It sets a political course in which the base remains the education establishment and not the larger public or school children and families. And it relies on the promise of an ever-expanding and inclusive "knowledge economy" to sustain society's investment in its education workforce, when in fact the knowledge economy rests atop a pyramid of increased stratification and exclusive opportunities.

To make a really historic leap, the center leadership needs to more deeply understand its new social paradigm, and learn from the agenda and practice of its progressive wing. This is not just an ideological preference or an obsession with education's belea-guered equity goals. What's most wrong with schools today, what makes them most vulnerable to the Right's war of attrition, is a crisis of inequality coupled with a failure to establish a holistic and systemic change process. The models and experience exist within the teacher unions to take steps forward in both arenas, but they will not carry the day from the sidelines.

The stakes are very high. There is no more powerful force defending public education today than the teacher unions, but they are still trapped between eras and identities. The hesitation to grasp a new identity in the merger is only symptomatic. Even with a merger, the unions cannot succeed without linking the future of the teaching profession with the future of all the nation's children. **TTU**

KATHY SLOANE

ANN BASTIAN IS A SENIOR PROGRAM OFFICER AT THE NEW WORLD FOUNDATION AND HAS WORKED WITHIN BOTH TEACHER UNIONS AS AN EDUCATION POLICY CONSULTANT ON ISSUES OF SCHOOL RESTRUCTURING AND COALITION BUILDING. SHE IS CO-AUTHOR OF *CHOOSING EQUALITY: THE CASE FOR DEMOCRATIC SCHOOLING*.

THIS ARTICLE WAS ORIGINALLY COMMISSIONED BY *NEW LABOR FORUM* AND APPEARED IN THEIR FALL 1998 ISSUE, WITH A RESPONSE FROM AN AFT LOCAL PRESIDENT. IT WAS PRINTED IN THE FALL 1998 ISSUE (VOL. 13, NO. 1) OF *RETHINKING SCHOOLS*.

Principles of Unity for a United Organization

During the spring and summer of 1998, members of the NEA and AFT hotly debated the matter of unity. Below are excerpts from the unity document that was considered by both organizations. These principles continue to influence ongoing merger discussions at the state level between NEA and AFT affiliates.

Our Mission

Three years ago, negotiators from the American Federation of Teachers and the National Education Association set out in a renewed effort to create a united institution.

From the beginning, leaders of both groups envisioned a new organization of men and women dedicated to providing a quality education for every child in America. An organization embodying the highest ideals and aspirations of its members. An organization willing to question familiar assumptions and explore new ideas. An organization better, not just bigger, than either the AFT or NEA alone.

Such an organization has been the goal of AFT and NEA policy for more than a generation. The elected representatives of both organizations now have the opportunity to make this vision a reality.

The AFT and NEA are both strong and successful institutions. Our success in building thoughtful, democratic organizations of educators has created an enduring legacy and transformed the lives of millions of children. Our work has attracted to both organizations professional and technical employees in health care and state and local government who have, in turn, helped us achieve goals important to our common future.

Today, we must all work together, as never before. Our accomplishments, as separate organizations, stand threatened. Our members face unprecedented assaults on public education and public service — and increasingly fierce attacks on their rights as working Americans.

Together, in a new United Organization, we can

KATHY SLOANE

benefit from the wisdom, talent, and experience of AFT and NEA members the nation over.

Together, we can devote more energy to preserving America's schools — the public schools — joining with those who would also transform them to meet the challenging needs of a changing age.

Together, united in a reinvigorated labor movement, we can more effectively advance the cause of economic and social justice and civil and human rights.

Together, we can better serve America's children and those who educate them, strengthening democracy in our schools, in our workplaces, and in our nation.

Principle One

The United Organization will champion public education.

Free, universal public education — America's great contribution to democracy — succeeds when all citizens accept responsibility for its success. The United Organization will welcome, at every level, help in ensuring every child a quality public school. Toward that end:

• The United Organization will forge partnerships to help eliminate the inequities that deny students a safe and supportive learning environment.

• The United Organization will help members share and perfect their professional skills and insist on high standards throughout the education profession.

• The United Organization will devote substantial resources toward identifying and promoting practices and strategies that enhance student achievement.

Principle Two

Education will be the United Organization's core membership jurisdiction.

The United Organization will be deeply committed to improving the well-being of members and the communities they serve. The UO will help affiliates in all jurisdictions maintain their current organizations and organize new members. ...

Principle Three

The United Organization will reach decisions democratically.

The United Organization created by the AFT and NEA will reflect a deep commitment to democratic principles and procedures — at every level. Members will run the United Organization. ...

Principle Four

The United Organization will strongly support affiliate efforts to serve members.

State and local affiliates will be the foundation of the United Organization. States and locals will provide most basic services to members and will receive substantial support from the national organization. ...

Principle Five

The United Organization will provide the highest quality services to members.

To become effective advocates for quality education, the members of the United Organization will need support from every level of the new organization. Both the AFT Organizational Assistance Program and the NEA UniServ program have served members well. The United Organization will help affiliates build upon these and other current services and break new ground to improve service quality. ...

Principle Six

The United Organization will foster diversity.

No institution in American life can do more to build respect for diversity than public education. The

United Organization will strive to become a model for the nation that educators are working to create. Toward that end:

• The United Organization will maintain — and work to expand — current AFT and NEA levels of minority representation throughout leadership, governance, and staff.

• The United Organization will promote programs and adopt policies designed to involve ethnic minority members in UO activities and decision making.

• United Organization governing bodies will be expandable, a capability that will make possible enhanced ethnic minority representation.

• The United Organization will adopt an employment program designed to recruit and employ ethnic minority staff members at all levels of the organization.

Principle Seven

The United Organization will work for a strong, democratic, and effective labor movement.

The well-being of America's children and families demands the economic and social justice that only a strong, democratic labor movement can provide. The United Organization shall be committed to building an effective, modern labor presence in American life. Toward that end:

• The United Organization will be a national affiliate of the AFL-CIO.

• The United Organization will work to build a strong, unified labor movement and endeavor to strengthen organized labor at the national, state, and local levels.

• The United Organization's initial affiliation with the national AFL-CIO will be based on 1.4 million members, a level that will make the United Organization the largest single affiliate within the AFL-CIO. ...

Principle Eight

The United Organization unification process will involve members and respect the past.

The launching of a new national organization must actively involve the men and women AFT and NEA members have elected to represent them. The United Organization will be created through a process that respects the democratic traditions and heritage of both organizations. TTU

— May 1, 1998

The New NEA: Reinventing Teacher Unions

BY BOB CHASE

The following is excerpted from a speech by NEA President Bob Chase, before the National Press Club on Feb. 5, 1997.

I CAME HERE THIS AFTERNOON TO INTRODUCE THE NEW National Education Association — the new union we are striving to create in public education. I am not shy about my plans to redirect our great association in big ways. Nor am I naive about the magnitude of this challenge.

Bear in mind that, for nearly three decades now, the National Education Association has been a traditional, somewhat narrowly focused union. We have butted heads with management over bread-and-butter issues — to win better salaries, benefits, and working conditions for school employees. And we have succeeded.

Today, however, it is clear to me — and to a critical mass of teachers across America — that while this narrow, traditional agenda remains important, it is utterly inadequate to meet the needs of the future. It will not serve our members' interest in greater professionalism. It will not serve the public's interest in better-quality public schools. And it will not serve the interests of America's children, the children we teach, the children who motivated us to go into teaching in the first place.

And this larger interest must be decisive. After all, America's public schools do not exist for teachers and other employees. They do not exist to provide us with jobs and salaries. Schools do exist for the children — to give students the very best, beginning with a quality teacher in every classroom.

Ladies and gentlemen, the imperative now facing public education could not be more stark. Simply put, in the decade ahead we must revitalize our public schools from within or they will be dismantled from without. And I am not talking here about the critics on talk radio who seek higher ratings by bashing public education and trashing teachers. I am talking about the vast majority of Americans who support public education but are clearly dissatisfied. They want higher-quality public schools, and they want them now.

To this end, we aim not so much to redirect NEA as to reinvent it. Yes, reinvention is a tall order. But we know we can do it because we did it once before. In the 1960s, we took a rather quiet, genteel professional association of educators, and we reinvented it as an

KATHY SLOANE

assertive — and, when necessary, militant — labor union.

But here is a critical point: When we reinvented our association in the 1960s, we modeled it after traditional industrial unions. Likewise, we accepted the industrial premise — namely, that labor and management have distinct, conflicting roles and interests, that we are destined to clash, that the union-management relationship is inherently adversarial.

Yes, these traditional industrial-style teacher unions have brought major improvements to public education: We have won smaller class sizes and better conditions for teaching and learning. We have also fought for decent salaries to attract and retain qualified teachers. And we have put our money where our mouth is when it comes to school reform. Over the past decade, NEA has spent some $70 million on reform initiatives — most recently, sponsoring six charter schools across the country.

The National Education Association is proud of the major improvements we have won in public education. However, these gains have been inadequate. And, too often, they have been won through confrontation at the bargaining table or, in extreme cases, after bitter strikes.

Which brings me to the crux of my message today. These industrial-style, adversarial tactics simply are not suited to the next stage of school reform. After much soul-searching and self-criticism within NEA, we know that it's time to create a new union — an association with an entirely new approach to our members, to our critics, and to our colleagues on the other side of the bargaining table. But to clear the air, I must publicly speak some rather blunt truths.

The fact is that while the vast majority of teachers are capable and dedicated professionals who put children's interests first, there are indeed some bad teachers in America's schools. And it is our job as a union to improve those teachers or, failing that, to get them out of the classroom.

Teacher Responsibility

While some of NEA's critics aim only to dismantle public education, many others care deeply about our schools, and we have been too quick to dismiss their criticisms and their ideas for change. The fact is that, in some instances, we have used our power to block uncomfortable changes, to protect the narrow interest of our members, and not to advance the interests of students and schools.

The fact is that while NEA does not control curriculum, set funding levels, or hire and fire, we cannot go on denying responsibility for school quality. We can't wash our hands of it and say, "that's management's job." School quality — the quality of the environment where students learn and where our members work — must be our responsibility as a union.

The fact is that, while the majority of NEA members teach in successful, for the most part suburban schools, we have been wrong to ignore the plight of inner-city schools. And to rectify this wrong, we have convened an Emergency Commission on Urban Children to put NEA foursquare in the fight to save urban children and their schools.

The fact is that, too often, NEA has sat on the sidelines of change, quick to say what won't work and slow to say what will. It is time for our great association to lead the reform, to engineer change, to take the initiative, to be in the vanguard.

NEA President Bob Chase.

And, on that score, the fact is that no group knows more about the solutions that will work in our schools than America's teachers. We know what our schools need: higher academic standards; stricter discipline; an end to social promotions; less bureaucracy; more resources where they count, in the classroom; schools that are richly connected to parents and to the communities that surround them.

To an amazing degree, teachers, school boards, and administrators all agree on this reform agenda. And this commonality cries out for us to build an entirely new union/management relationship in public education.

Our challenge is clear. Instead of relegating teachers to the role of production workers, with no say in organizing their schools for excellence, we need to enlist teachers as full partners, indeed, as co-managers of their schools. Instead of contracts that reduce flexibility and restrict change, we — and our schools — need contracts that empower and enable.

Many traditionalists within NEA, predictably, have difficulty accepting this new unionism. They say that what I propose is a threat to union clout and solidarity. To which I give a direct answer: This new collaboration is not about sleeping with the enemy. It is about waking up to our shared stake in reinvigorating the public education enterprise. It is about educating children better, more effectively, more ambitiously.

Permit me to add a personal note here. I well understand the traditional union view that says a union's job is strictly "to look out for me." I understand it because I once held this view myself.

In 1983, after the *Nation at Risk* report came out, NEA President Mary Hatwood Futrell tried to mobilize our union to lead the reform movement in American public education. At the time, as a member of NEA's executive committee, I took a leading role in opposing her. I argued that we should stick to our knitting — stick to bargaining for better pay and working conditions.

That, ladies and gentlemen, was the biggest mistake of my career. I was wrong. And today, with all due respect, I say to the traditionalists in NEA's ranks, to those who argue that we should stick to our knitting, leaving education reform to others: You are mistaken.

I also say — I insist — that the new course we have charted at NEA is not strictly about vision. As British Prime Minister Harold Macmillan said long ago: "If you want a vision, consult a saint. I am a politician." And so it is with me. I am a teacher whose heart and soul are still in the classroom; I still instinctively check for chalk smudges on my clothes. I am also a commit-

ted unionist; a veteran of more hard-fought collective bargaining sessions than I can remember. I deal in practical, concrete, tangible changes. I deal in results.

The new direction we are charting at NEA is not only about vision; it is about action. It is about changing how each of our local affiliates does business, changing how they bargain, changing what issues they put on the table, changing the ways they help their members to become the best teachers they can be.

I repeat, the new NEA is about action. And, on that score, I challenge the American public: Watch what we do, not what we say.

Our new directions are clear: putting issues of school quality front and center at the bargaining table,

---

No group knows more about the solutions that will work in our schools than America's teachers.

---

collaborating actively with management on an agenda of school reform, involving teachers and other school employees in organizing their schools for excellence.

The good news is that teachers on the front line are already advancing this agenda. They are way ahead of NEA's leadership. Indeed, my motto as NEA president should be: I am their leader; I must follow them.

For example, imagine a future where teachers, under their union contract, have responsibility for nearly three-quarters of a school system's budget, and they use that authority to cut class sizes and boost academic quality. Well, that future is now. I just described the work of our local union in New Albany, Indiana.

Or imagine the president of a local NEA union taking the lead in founding a public charter school, a new school that she and her colleagues manage by themselves, without a principal. I just described the work of Jan Noble, president of our affiliate in Colorado Springs.

By any measure, these are bold new arrangements. But a growing number of NEA teachers insist on going one step further. They argue that it's not enough to cooperate with management on school reform. Quality must begin at home, within our own ranks. If a teacher is not measuring up in the classroom, if there is a bad teacher in one of our schools, then we must do something about it.

Political Risk

To the traditional unionists who say that this is heresy and a threat to union solidarity, I say: Come

Industrial-style, adversarial tactics simply are not suited to the next stage of school reform. After much soul-searching and self-criticism within NEA, we know that it's time to create a new union — an association with an entirely new approach to our members, to our critics, and to our colleagues on the other side of the bargaining table.

visit our NEA local in Columbus, Ohio. The Columbus Education Association designates senior teachers to serve as full-time consultants in the classroom. They intervene to help veteran teachers whose skills need sharpening. In most cases, this intervention is successful. But in roughly 10% of cases, the consultants — members of our union — take the lead in counseling a

problem teacher to leave the profession. If necessary, they recommend dismissal. This is work that entails real political risk for teacher/leaders within their local unions. I believe it is exactly the right course for the new NEA.

At the end of the 19th century, labor pioneer Samuel Gompers famously stated the goal of his union in one word: "More!" Today, entering a new era, teachers are setting forth another goal for their unions: Better!

So let me state categorically what NEA will do:

• To parents and the public, NEA pledges to work with you to ensure that every classroom in America has a quality teacher. This means we accept our responsibility to assist in removing teachers — that small minority of teachers — who are unqualified, incompetent, or burned out.

• To the business community, NEA pledges to work with you to raise and enforce standards for student achievement, to ensure that high school graduates are — at a minimum — literate, competent in the basic skills, equipped for the workplace.

• To President Clinton and the Congress, we at NEA pledge our enthusiastic support for the extraordinary agenda — a truly 21st-century agenda for children and education — set forth in last night's State of the Union address.

• To school boards and administrators, NEA pledges to engage you in a new partnership — at the bargaining table and in our day-to-day relationship — aimed at transforming the quality of our schools.

• And to those who seek genuinely to reform public education — and not to dismantle it — NEA pledges to join with you to challenge the entrenched system, to fight for the changes that we know are urgent and necessary.

These are our pledges.

I have absolute confidence that we can build the new NEA I have described for you this afternoon. What's more, I have absolute confidence that this new NEA can be a driving force — I hope the driving force — in revitalizing public education for America's children. **TTU**

KATHY SLOANE

FOR A COPY OF THE COMPLETE SPEECH VISIT: WWW.NEA.ORG/NR/SP970205.HTML.

Whither Public Education?

BY SANDRA FELDMAN

The following are excerpts from the keynote address delivered by Sandra Feldman, President of the American Federation of Teachers, at the AFT 1998 Convention, July 17, 1998, New Orleans, Louisiana.

As A UNION, WE KNOW THAT THE QUESTION IS NO longer "whither public education?" We can handle that. We know that big changes are necessary, and we're ready, willing, and able to make them, even if it means doing things very differently; we and our members have always been willing to embrace change — so long as it carries forward the cherished ideals of public education and our democracy, so long as it helps this nation make good on them.

But the question we're hearing isn't "whither public education" but "whether" — a question never raised before in America. That it could be asked at all is stunning. That the answer could be "no" has consequences too terrible to contemplate.

So let me say to the privatization demagogues: Our opposition to vouchers, to putting education on a market basis, is not out of narrow union interest. It is not about losing members. In fact, we have lots of reasons to believe we'd organize and grow. No, our opposition to vouchers is out of our interest in children and democracy!

It is because we do not believe for a minute that our public schools are hopeless or that a market system of education would work. We do not believe that it could deliver opportunity and quality to the vast majority of Americans, or that it offers the best hope for poor children, or that it would preserve and strengthen our democracy.

And we will fight to the last against putting the education of our children on a market basis — as if our children were no more than fast food — because the worst public schools in America today would look good compared to what a market system of schools would usher in!

And it's because our democracy cannot stand if all our children do not have an absolute right to get educated. Remember: Education is first and foremost about the capacity to safeguard our liberties. If educating our children depends on a roll of the dice and the condition of some school entrepreneur's bottom line, then this country cannot be the kind of democracy we've cherished and always strived to improve!

This is what our union stands against. And we're proud of it!

But the plain fact is, the dangerous forces gathering in our country couldn't be getting the audience they're getting if there weren't some deep problems in our institutions, problems that are as discernible to parents and the public as they are to us.

For the sake of everything we believe in and the good this country stands for, we've got to keep on working — even harder and smarter. That goes for the national, our locals, and our state affiliates — every level of the union.

So we're going to be even more aggressive in taking our case — the case for children — to parents and the public. Because the common-sense solutions they seek are exactly what we seek and know how to achieve.

And we must take the lead with superintendents and school boards, mayors, and governors. We won't wait for them to ask for our help in turning around our schools. We'll get to them first with our knowledge, experience, and creativity.

And we must be tenacious. If they turn us down, as some have done, for very poor reasons, we'll go back, again and again — with parents and other allies behind us — to press our case for children.

We must do everything within our power to make turning around low-performing schools — improving all schools — the top agenda of every community in this nation! And we will do it in the common-sense ways the public, parents, our members, and the research all support.

Now, having said that, it also must be said that, while there are serious problems, the idea that all our public schools are failing is simply wrong, terribly wrong. It's demagoguery, pure and simple.

You know, most parents — and I'll get to the important exceptions later — are satisfied with their children's schools. And I think it's because most parents know first hand that their kids are getting a very good education. They see how dedicated and hard-working teachers are. They see teachers stepping into the breach created by stressed-out parents and the lack of community activities for children, from our suburbs to our inner cities. And they know their children are learning.

Could we be doing better? Absolutely. But the idea that we have a failing public school system is simply outrageous.

The same goes for the charge that all the public schools serving poor children are failing, or that we've made no progress since "A Nation at Risk."

The plain truth is that, thanks to you, our children, including our poor children, have made great progress.

Just a few weeks ago, in a report that got little attention, the Census Bureau found that 86 percent of young blacks between the ages of 25 and 29 were high school graduates — 86 percent compared to 87 percent of whites. That's a statistically insignificant difference. That's tremendous progress! In 1965, it was 50 percent of blacks and 73 percent of whites.

Education reform is working! Academic standards and requirements are up, student attendance is up, dropout rates are down, and our students are achieving at much higher levels.

And what is particularly extraordinary is that we've

AP/WIDE WORLD PHOTOS

AFT President Sandra Feldman.

taken our children this far despite America's childhood poverty rate — I repeat, the highest in the industrialized world. We've taken our children this far even though entry-level wages for male high school graduates, for example, fell 28 percent from 1973 to 1997. And even the prosperous times during this period didn't stop the free fall. And we know that while our children may not know these statistics, they know very well that even if they do everything right, their future may not include a living wage.

The progress of our children and public schools is amazing, especially given the economic circumstances. It's astonishing, given the lack of support teachers endure and the awful neglect so many of our students suffer. And our progress ought to make us proud and all Americans hopeful. Because if we've come this far — notwithstanding poverty, vicious politics, and persistent efforts to keep this nation from carrying out the reforms that really work — think of what could be accomplished if our elected leaders and school authorities really got serious about putting reform in place!

Now, we in the AFT are second to none in caring about a first-rate education for all our kids! And we are second to none on high standards and the work we've done to bring them to realization. And we have never covered up the bad news about our schools; quite the opposite.

So let me say this bluntly. The work on improving our public schools is far from done. And it is not moving far and fast enough.

We cannot be content, even with the performance of our advantaged kids, because they and their schools could be doing much better.

And, most especially and emphatically, we cannot be content that there are many public schools where poor children are doing very well. Because, despite substantial progress, the gap in achievement between advantaged and poor children continues to be unacceptable. And we cannot be content while too many poor parents are dissatisfied with their children's schools.

Remember: There is a concerted effort going on in this country to convince Americans that leaving the majority of kids behind is an act of kindness rather than an assault on children, that our only obligation to poor children is to select a handful of the so-called "deserving poor," leave them to the mercies of a lottery, and to hell with the rest.

The battle against this cynical idea, this abandonment of a future for each and every child, is a battle that can't be won only in the political arena — though we intend to redouble our efforts at political action.

But the ultimate weapon, the only enduring way to win, is to raise all children's achievement and to close the achievement gap, to make every school a school we'd gladly send our own children to.

So, together, we're going to commit to increasing the number of locals that are concentrating on turning around low-performing schools.

We're going to push harder to equip all our locals, our schools, and our members with the information and tools necessary to do what works for children.

The fact is, this nation doesn't have to choose between teacher quality or the individual rights of teachers, which also protects teacher quality. We need to do both. We can do both.

Despite substantial progress, the gap in achievement between advantaged and poor children continues to be unacceptable. And we cannot be content while too many poor parents are dissatisfied with their children's schools.

So let me propose a partnership on behalf of teacher quality. Because, again, we can't do it alone — and political and school officials have certainly demonstrated they can't do it.

First, instead of capitalizing on dismissal proceedings that are time consuming, costly, inefficient, and more adversarial than professional, let's streamline them and professionalize them, as we've already done in a number of states and districts. Let's use these model laws and contracts.

Second, instead of blaming seniority rules for all the ills of the world and proposing to give principals sole discretion over hiring, let's treat teachers as professionals and involve them in the hiring process. Instead of trying to end rules established to protect against arbitrary and capricious decisions, let's make sure that a teacher's qualifications and demonstrated fit with a school's educational philosophy or program are what count. We have such schools. We have contract language that achieves this goal.

Third, instead of capitalizing on lousy, top-down teacher evaluation systems that make it too easy to get tenured, that are indifferent about teachers who are falling down on the job and offer no assistance to teachers who need help, let's negotiate a peer review and intervention program. Because believe me, no one is more knowledgeable and rigorous about teacher performance than first-rate teachers!

We pioneered peer review and intervention. Many of our locals are doing it. It works, not only in our eyes but according to the experts on teacher evaluation. Yet negotiation is a two-way street. We can't ram even the most effective programs down management's throat; believe me, we've tried. Let's negotiate.

Fourth, instead of allowing new teachers to sink or swim, let's set up teacher internship programs. They work. Yes, they cost money. But those costs are nothing compared to the cost of the talent we lose in the first, difficult year of teaching because no one is there to help. Those costs are nothing compared to the education that's lost to children when the new strug- gling teachers they happen to have are sinkers rather than swimmers.

Fifth, make schools learning communities for teachers, as well as for students. Provide for master teachers, teacher centers, real professional development in the schools — with time for teachers to work with one another to overcome children's learning problems as they come up.

My last point is really the first. Because, our teacher quality problem is far more of a future problem than a current one. Our teaching force is "maturing." We are on our way to replacing two million teachers. Who will these new teachers be?

The truth is, in places that have the toughest conditions and pay the least — translation: the schools serving our poorest, neediest children — teaching standards aren't the problem. The problem is the chronic undermining of those standards through "emergency" credentials and misassignment of teachers to classes they aren't trained to teach. That's our teacher quality problem!

Let's face it. Emergency licenses and teacher misassignment have created a structural teacher quality deficit in this country. And this ought to be taken as seriously as the budget deficit has been.

And the elimination or lowering of standards for entry into the profession in any school, including charter schools or voucher schools, can only make it worse.

So let me repeat my challenge to state and local education authorities: If you're really serious about teacher quality, stop undercutting even the standards we have now. Stop creating and perpetuating a struc- tural teacher quality deficit into the next century. This school year, put an end to emergency credentials and the misassignment of teachers.

This is not a proposal lightly made. Because if it is implemented, we would have a crisis in many schools. I should say, a more visible, more difficult-to-deal-with crisis than we have at present. Because we would have many classrooms throughout some of our cities that go not only without teachers, but without babysitters. And the structural teacher quality deficit would be shamefully exposed.

But we cannot allow this problem to continue. And we cannot allow state and local education authorities, and others, to get off the hook with talk about how they can't precipitate a crisis. Like I said, this already is a crisis, especially for our neediest children.

So, to avoid any excuses — and because it's the right thing for us to do — I also call on our affiliates and on our members to help get through such a crisis by negotiating ways to accommodate the additional shortages until qualified teachers are found.

Let us provide what the millions upon millions of children need and deserve in America — free and equal access to high-quality public education.

This is my challenge to those who run public education — the state and local officials, the boards of education, the superintendents — and to our own local and state unions:

Measure every school by the highest standard: Would I want my own child to be there?

And, in addition to all the other school improve- ment efforts we are making and working on together — high standards, good discipline, programs that work — together, let's take this basic step: enforce high entry standards into the teaching profession, so that as we face the next century, the children of America — no matter their parents' wealth, no matter the wealth or status of their neighborhood — have truly equal access to this essential element of a good education: well-educated, qualified teachers in their classrooms.

I believe this great country of ours will face up to the challenges before us and do the right thing for children, families, and all Americans. I know that our great union will continue to pursue our proud and worthy tradition. TTU

Organizing
for the Future

Defending the Public Sector

AN INTERVIEW WITH LABOR ACTIVIST BILL FLETCHER

The following is from an interview with Bill Fletcher, director of education for the AFL-CIO. Fletcher has been involved in union organizing and reform for more than 20 years, in both public- and private-sector unions. He is also a long-time activist in the African-American community, and helped convene the Black Radical Congress in Chicago in 1998. Fletcher was interviewed by Bob Peterson.

struggles over decades. I would argue that many, if not most, of these functions cannot and should not be operated with the profit motive in mind.

Such services must be the concern of public-sector unions. Thus, this defense of the public sector goes way beyond a matter of job protection; it speaks to a defense of society itself.

Public-sector workers serve the public and are paid through tax dollars. They thus play a different role than autoworkers, steelworkers, or shipbuilders working for a private business. Given these differences, what special roles do public-sector unions play in society?

Public-sector unions play three roles. First, they defend the interests of their members. Second, and a lot of public-sector unions talk about this so much that it's almost a cliché, they must look out for the interests of the community. A third role, which is not talked about a lot in the United States but is discussed overseas, is that they must defend the public sector.

I feel this third role is critical right now. Public-sector unions need to articulate a coherent and credible defense of the public sector — to explain the role of the public sector and show why any kind of civilized society must have a public sector. I don't think public-sector unions do that very well. As a result, they tend to come across as merely defending the interests of their members.

When I speak about the "public sector," I am not just talking about government jobs. I am referring to the larger question of all public services and public space. For example, parks and recreational facilities are collective necessities which aim to improve peoples' quality of life and living standards. Many of these "spaces" and other public services were won through

One criticism of teacher unions is that they are part of a "government monopoly" — that public education is better served through privatization and other mechanisms to spur competition. What do you think?

The notion that the private sector is somehow more efficient is a complete fallacy. There are plenty of historical examples, for example the railroads. Why did railroads become part of the public sector? Because they were destroyed by private-sector interests. Why did the subway system in New York City, which had been run by three private companies, become a quasi-public agency? Because they were being destroyed by the companies.

Public-sector unions have to expose that kind of history. But we also need to talk about the fact that there are things necessary for a civilized society that cost money and may not always result in a profit. For example, there is a social cost of not having a mass

---

Public-sector unions need to articulate a coherent and credible defense to explain why any kind of civilized society must have a public sector.

---

transportation system, particularly in large cities, and this social cost is more damaging than running metropolitan transportation systems at a loss. As a result, in many urban areas there is a social investment that helps subsidize mass transit.

What happens when there's a budget crunch and talk of reductions in mass transit? Unfortunately, too often the public-sector union will merely emphasize the number of jobs lost. Well, that's the wrong time to be fighting the battle. Public-sector unions need to be talking, before the crisis erupts, about the role of the public sector, and they need to be building coalition with community-based organizations well before the budget crunch hits. They need to go on the offensive in defense of the public sector.

Can you think of an example when a public-sector union took that initiative to form a community/labor alliance when it wasn't just in their narrow self-interest?

No, though there are probably some which I am overlooking. To be honest, most of the examples I can think of all took place when it was crunch time and there was some sort of threat. That crunch time has

arrived for public education, so to speak, and the time is ripe for a community/labor alliance.

In the Black community, there has traditionally been strong support for public schools. But there is utter frustration with some schools, and so there is growing support for vouchers. The question, it seems to me, is what role the teacher unions can play in elaborating a credible reform proposal for urban schools.

Some people argue that workers should be wary of collaborating with managers and bosses. At the same time, others such as NEA President Bob Chase argue for a form of "new unionism" that involves increased collaboration with the administration. What's your view on labor/management collaboration?

Terms such as labor/management collaboration have become very loaded, so I prefer to talk about issues such as "worker participation." It's important to look at the substance of the proposal, not simply the form and rhetoric.

For example, every time a union signs a collective bargaining agreement with an employer, it is agreeing to cooperate. That's a reality. It's actually part of the reason the Industrial Workers of the World (IWW) wouldn't sign collective bargaining agreements.

The labor movement has rejected the IWW approach, and recognizes that in a collective bargaining agreement, we are agreeing to cooperate on certain things. To me, the question is not so much one of cooperation, but the terms of the discussions. How is the cooperation being done? Is it designed to take advantage of the workers' knowledge — but at the workers' expense? Is it designed to circumvent or undermine the union? Those are the types of issues that need to be looked at.

Unions also need to challenge what are seen as management rights: issues such as the future of enterprise, the quality of the product, how best to serve the customer, investment decisions. These are all things that workers should have a say in, not necessarily as individuals but collectively through their union.

When you talk about public arenas such as public transportation or public schools, the unions should be a way for the rank-and-file workers to get involved in such discussions. If we want to be candid, we have to recognize that part of the problem is that many unions do not have way for rank-and-filers to become involved, and then the workers become alienated from their union and, on an individual level, much more susceptible to management's view.

Historically, teachers have vacillated between viewing themselves as professionals — who want individual control over working conditions — and as workers who see the need for collective action. What would you say to those who think teachers should be treated as professionals and are hesitant about being associated with "blue-collar unionism"?

I think teachers should be treated and respected as professionals, because they are. But being professional shouldn't be seen as being superior.

I come out of the industrial union mode of thinking on these questions, and tend to think that wall-to-wall is the best way to build power. It's not about whether teachers like janitors or janitors like teachers. The question is: How do you strengthen the power of the workers?

This issue is very much related to the question, which has come up in both the AFT and NEA, about who should be in the bargaining unit. I think that is a tactical matter that should be settled on the basis of an analysis of power. It's also a question of how you go about building a sense of identity.

In many cities, teacher unions are predominantly white while the students are predominantly students of color. What are the implications of this for teacher unions?

When I was going through school, some of the most important teachers for me were white. I will forever be in their debt. But having said that, I think that when students do not see people who look like them in positions of authority, this reinforces white supremacy and reinforces feelings of being "the other." Further, from the standpoint of pedagogy, you need to have a teaching workforce that resembles the student population.

And the implications for unions?

Teacher unions need to become involved in recruitment and employment issues. They need to argue for affirmative action and for the recruitment of teachers who look like and understand the issues of the student population. That's the minimum.

But it also means, and this is a little dicier, that the entire workforce has to be sensitive to race, class, and gender dynamics. And this must go beyond cultural awareness. More important, it means understanding the history of racism and the many ways racism manifests itself. The same is true for sexism and class issues.

Class is generally not discussed in schools. If it comes up, it is brief, and usually in the context of

comments such as, "Oh yea, by the way, there's a labor movement." But there is rarely any discussion of the psychological impact of class. In fact, class is one of these forbidden words in the English language.

I think that teacher unions have an obligation to demand regular training programs or institutes in these issues, and that teachers should get continuing education credits for attending them.

Whether or not they merge, what role do you think the AFT and NEA can play in the future of the American labor movement?

Teachers help to shape the minds of the future generation. One important role is help build awareness about unions and the labor movement. Some teachers don't want to talk to their students about unions; they see it as somehow unethical and misusing their

---

The notion that the private sector is somehow more efficient is a complete fallacy. There are plenty of historical examples, such as the railroads. Why did railroads become part of the public sector? Because they were destroyed by private-sector interests.

---

position. That's ridiculous. Teachers need to help sow the seeds of the future of unionism.

Teacher unions also can play a pivotal role in fighting back against the attack on the public sector. A couple of years ago, I was talking with some teacher-union officials about the attack on public education. I argued that they were absolutely right to raise this alarm, but that they needed to do so in the context of the overall attack on the public sector. They looked at me as if I were an alien from *Star Trek*. They stared and said, "Yea, but we really have to defend public education."

I replied that if the public sector is destroyed, or the concept is so diminished that it's meaningless, then there will be no public education to defend. That's not to say we should ignore the specific importance of defending public education, but rather to emphasize that the attack is occurring in the context of an attack on the very premise of the importance of a public sector. TTU

The Strength of the Public Sector

BY BOB CHASE

NO AMOUNT OF FAITH IN THE MARKET CAN OVER-rule the cold truth of this matter: The market cannot handle the education of 46.6 million children in 87,125 K-12 public schools, in 14,471 school districts across the country ....

Granted, the market is an incredibly dynamic force in our society, and we should give it room to do what it does best. But profits are not the measure of all that is good in our lives. There are certain tasks — educating most of our children, cleaning up our waters and our air, insuring the safety of our food supply, conserving our national parks and forests, defending our nation, exploring outer space, and ... protecting us from fire — that the public sector must take responsibility for, or they *will not get done.*

These are all tasks, you may note, that require something more than millions of individuals consumers, satisfying their individual appetite for decaf, skinny, mocha, vanilla latté or whatever. These are tasks that require individuals coming together with other individuals and putting their shoulders to the commonweal.

Americans have always been impatient with the public

The notion that market competition will save the public schools in communities already abandoned by the market strains credulity.

sector, demanding of it the same degree of efficiency we expect in the market. This is a healthy tendency in our political culture, but it sometimes leads us to forget or overlook the genuine accomplishments of the public sector.

It was the *public* health vaccination effort that eradicated smallpox and polio in the United States — and it will be a *public* health vaccination effort that will someday soon, I pray, eradicate AIDS.

In science and technology, it was the *public* sector that developed the basic technology that underpins the Internet. It was *public* sector-funded research that sparked the rapid development of the mighty microchip. Plus, it is the *public* sector's patent protection that ensures inventors will profit from their hard work. The bottom-line-driven market can be very shortsighted, while the *public* sector can take the longer view, investing, for example, in basic scientific research. If we don't let ideology get in the way, the public sector's strengths can complement the market's weaknesses, just as the market can complement the public sector.

And in poor neighborhoods and communities, it is the *public* sector that continues to provide basic human services long after the market has abandoned them. The big-name banks and supermarkets and hardware stores may have pulled out of the places where low-income people live, but the public schools are still there.

The notion that market competition, and only market competition, will save the public schools in communities already abandoned by the market strains credulity. TTU

EXCERPTED FROM A SPEECH GIVEN IN LOS ANGELES ON FEBRUARY 18, 1999. FOR THE FULL TEXT, SEE: WWW.NEA.ORG/NR/SP990218.HTML. BOB CHASE IS PRESIDENT OF THE NEA.

The Market Is Not the Answer

AN INTERVIEW WITH JONATHAN KOZOL

The very word "public" has a negative connotation these days. How does one counter that negative image in a way that one can defend public schools but not defend the status quo?

We've got to be blunt about the problems in a public system and be harsh critics of those problems. We don't want to be in the position of knee-jerk defenders of the public schools against the bad guys.

But we have to be careful not to succumb to this nonsense that a public system is inherently flawed and that therefore we have to turn to the marketplace for solutions. I've never in my entire life seen any evidence that the competitive free market, unrestricted, without a strong counterpoise within the public sector, will ever dispense decent medical care, sanitation, transportation, or education to the people. It's as simple as that.

I think it's time for us to begin to look back at some of our roots as Americans. It's absolutely crucial to claim the high moral ground on this issue and make it clear that the right-wing voucher advocates are subverting a strong American tradition. In this respect, we are the defenders of American history.

Let me state it differently. The complaints about the apparent malfunction of the public system are linked, in my belief, to the peculiar problems of impoverished, often virtually colonized, urban school

JEAN-CLAUDE LEJEUNE

> **I've never in my entire life seen any evidence that the competitive free market, unrestricted, will ever dispense decent medical care, sanitation, transportation, or education to the people.**

systems. I mean "colonized" in the sense that very little power actually exists within the system, least of all the most important power which is finance, for which they're dependent on outside forces. And those outside forces are the people who set tax rates, the state government, the federal government, and the people who shape economic policy in America. I don't think the problems in urban public schools are inherently those of public education. I see hundreds of fine suburban school systems all around the country where nobody ever raises any question about the dangers of monopoly, because these are well-funded, reasonably attractive school systems.

Monopoly Not the Problem

I think it's important to recognize that this issue of monopoly never came up until people realized the incredible problems of our segregated, impoverished, colonized inner-city systems, and needed to find a scapegoat other than segregation and colonization. The issue to me is not that these are public institutions. The issue is that these city schools are basically powerless. The superintendent is usually the viceroy representing other interests to which the superintendent has to be deferential, usually at great emotional cost.

My own faith leads me to defend the genuinely ethical purposes of public education as a terrific American tradition, and to point to what it's done at its best — not simply for the very rich, but for the average American citizen. We need to place the voucher advocates, the enemies of public schools, where they belong: in the position of those who are subverting something decent in America. **TTU**

JONATHAN KOZOL IS THE AUTHOR OF *SAVAGE INEQUALITIES, AMAZING GRACE,* AND OTHER BOOKS ON CHILDREN. THIS INTERVIEW BY THE EDITORS OF *RETHINKING SCHOOLS* ORIGINALLY APPEARED IN *FUNDING FOR JUSTICE: MONEY, EQUITY, AND THE FUTURE OF PUBLIC EDUCATION* (MILWAUKEE: RETHINKING SCHOOLS, 1997).

A Review of *United Mind Workers*

BY BOB PETERSON

United Mind Workers: Unions and Teaching in the Knowledge Society, by Charles Taylor Kerchner, Julia E. Koppich, and Joseph G. Weeres. (San Francisco: Jossey-Bass, 1997).

GIVEN THE CHALLENGES AND POSSIBILITIES FACING teacher unions, the new book, *United Mind Workers*, comes at a propitious time. Subtitled *Unions and Teaching in the Knowledge Society,* the book is by three education professors at California's Claremont Graduate Schools. They write, "This book is about teacher unions, not as they are, but as they might be."

The NEA sells a 50-page summary/study guide of the book. Adam Urbanski, President of the (AFT) Rochester Teachers Association, called the book a "timely and significant contribution. ... The thrust of the book is right on."

United Mind Workers covers a broad range of topics including educational standards, wages and benefits, evaluation and staff development, and other professional issues. In each case, the authors stretch traditional notions of unionism and advocate innovations. Even if only one-half of the authors' proposals were adopted, teacher unions would have a new "professional" character that would change how schools operate and how the public perceives teacher unions.

Despite its strengths, the book has significant problems. It lacks a coherent social analysis and seems to capitulate to aspects of a conservative, "free-market" approach to education. Moreover, while Kerchner and his colleagues do a stellar job detailing what teacher unions should do to become more "professional," their near silence on teacher unions and social justice is disappointing. More troubling, they never discuss the issue of race and teacher unionism.

Teachers As Experts

The authors staunchly support teacher unionism

yet are frank with their criticisms. They argue that teacher unions have done a good job organizing around issues of job control, work rules, and economic rights. The task at hand, they argue, is that unions must now organize around "the other half of teachers' jobs" — teachers as educators.

JEAN-CLAUDE LEJEUNE

"Defining and measuring quality — for students, for teachers, for schools — is central to what unions need to do," they argue.

The authors call teachers "unacknowledged experts," who know more about teaching and learning "than do governors, business leaders, and most college professors." But, they argue, collective bargaining has only legitimated teachers' economic interests and has never recognized them "as experts about learning."

Kerchner and colleagues identify an underlying phenomenon that they say necessitates a new approach for teacher unionism — the shift from what they call an "industrial society" to a "knowledge society." The authors also take up issues such as charters, privatization, and decentralization, implicitly underscoring the ideological shift away from centralized solutions towards local decision-making.

Peer review is not only a superior means of evaluation, they argue, but also is a means by which "teachers can describe their craft" — and change conversations among teachers and interactions between teachers, parents, students, and school administrators.

The book argues that teacher unions should focus organizing in three core areas:
- Quality of learning and teaching.
- School-based compacts.
- Teacher hiring and advancement.

Quality of Learning and Teaching

Unions should promote quality by becoming involved in rethinking teacher training and the teacher's job responsibilities, creating standards for student performance, and implementing peer assistance and review programs. Specific suggestions range from having unions promote teacher-based curriculum committees to developing flexible work hours so teachers have more time to reflect and work together outside of the classroom. Kerchner and colleagues strongly support national standards — calling them necessary because they define the central mission of education. They believe that teacher unions should put considerable resources into creating "a system of indicators of school accountability at the national and state levels" and into training members "to gather and interpret indicator data at the local level."

The authors are strong advocates of peer review, which they describe as "the process by which teachers assess the professional competence of their colleagues." They see peer review as an "essential quality lever" for schools. It is not only a superior means of evaluation, they argue, but also is a means by which "teachers can describe their craft" — and change conversations among teachers and interactions between teachers, parents, students, and school administrators. Using peer review, they argue, unions can assume responsibility for the quality of the teaching profession. The authors outline the peer review experience of Columbus, Ohio, that began in 1981 and that of Poway, California, two of a handful of districts that have begun to experiment with reform. After reading the authors' analysis, one is left to agree with Rochester Teachers' Association President Adam Urbanski, who says, "Peer review is only controversial where it hasn't been tried."

School-based Compacts

The authors believe that another key reform involves "differentiating among types and styles of schools." They lament that even though two million teachers belong to strong labor organizations, they have been unable to "develop workplaces built around collaboration and teamwork." To solve this problem, they propose that current contracts be replaced with a "slender central agreement setting forth consensually achieved educational goals" and coupled with "site-based compacts" that include community input. Under their scenario, "most of the decisions that lie at the heart of teaching and learning would shift to schools" — including hiring and letting go of teachers, setting schedules and work days, deciding on supplementary salaries, contracting out, and so forth. They acknowledge that in recent years there have been efforts to "loosen the constraints of the contract without losing the purpose of collective bargaining." But they believe that such reforms have been reduced in most instances "to sporadic flirtations with flexibility" and have been "fairly timid, focused on single issues and hamstrung by much of the same sort of tight procedural language and bureaucratic machinery that characterizes the contracts themselves."

Teacher Hiring and Advancement

One the authors' most intriguing ideas is to radically change how teachers are hired and placed in schools. They recognize that employment security was a hard-won right. But they distinguish between "job security," which they define as the granting of tenure in one district, and "career security," which is based on the idea of portable benefits and pensions which would allow teachers to move from district to district or state to state without losing financially. They envision unions establishing "electronic hiring halls" and taking over the role of most personnel offices of local school districts. Such "hiring halls" would be patterned after hiring halls of longshoremen and waitress unions. They would register applications, help applicants prepare portfolios, maintain an electronic database for its service area, and act as an employment broker.

Tied to their idea of "career security" are career ladders. Under their vision of career ladders, teachers who take on increased responsibilities in areas such as curriculum and staff development would get higher pay. The authors also write favorably about districts that pay more money to teachers who have gone through the National Board for Professional Teacher Standards certification (a questionable practice, in my mind). Further, they write that once individual schools have the right to develop their own "compacts," decisions to supplement a base teacher salary would be made based on a teacher's "demonstrated knowledge and skills." They dismiss concerns that such policies might enhance "unhealthy interpersonal competition." Instead, they argue, they would have "the effect of enhancing the ability of individual teachers or groups of teachers to be entrepreneurs, to market their specific complement of skills and talents to schools seeking these attributes."

Union Democracy

The book touches briefly on the issue of union democracy. At one point, the authors charge that "both unions, but the NEA in particular, develop conversational orthodoxies in which some subjects are virtually undiscussable. A serious outbreak of free speech

would be of great benefit." Later on they argue that "union structures are basically hierarchical, just like management structures, and prestige, influence, and attention flow upward. The building representative or steward is largely an afterthought, as is the functioning of the union at an individual school."

While some union leaders will disagree, internal democracy is a legitimate issue. Given the potential merger of the NEA and AFT, it is a particularly important time to discuss such matters. A strong dose of rank-and-file involvement can only strengthen the union, regardless of how increased democracy may affect some in local or national union leadership.

There has been a historic divide in many teacher unions between those who commit themselves to union activities and politics — an almost full-time occupation in addition to teaching, if one hopes to influence the union — and those who commit themselves to "professional teaching" practices such as starting innovative schools, leading district curriculum committees, or participating in state and national professional organizations. This historic division reinforces other pressures that keep teacher unions focused on issues of wages and hours. What gets lost, as a result, is a union emphasis on broader educational reforms. If teacher unions are serious about furthering quality education, they will have to devise ways to

JEAN-CLAUDE LEJEUNE

promote true union democracy and better involve teachers experienced in educational innovation and reform.

Free-Market Ideology

As a co-founder of an innovative inner-city public school in Milwaukee, I am sympathetic to the authors' contention that a lot of decision-making should be shifted to the school level. Interestingly, that same experience convinces me that some of the radical decentralization proposals put forth by Kerchner and his colleagues (and others whom they reference, such as Paul Hill) would be detrimental to local school-based operations. (See my article, "Total Decentralization: Contradictions and Dangers," *Rethinking Schools*, Vol. 9 #4). While I believe local schools should have considerable say over matters of budget, staffing, and

---

Proposals for such total decentralization may sound nice in theory but rarely come from classroom teachers who have been involved in decentralization for any length of time.

---

curricula, problems will emerge if local schools are responsible for staff bonuses, salaries or benefits, or contracting out matters such as food and janitorial services. I'm worried not just about the potential for patronage. More important, I know the incredible amount of time that such matters can consume, diverting attention from the key issues of teaching and learning.

Proposals for such total decentralization may sound nice in theory but rarely come from classroom teachers who have been involved in decentralization for any length of time. I believe that the book's perspective on school-based decision-making is rooted less in a commitment to grassroots democracy than in a capitulation to marketplace ideology and the onslaught of market-based reforms such as vouchers for private schools. (For a critique of the marketplace approach to education reform, see the *Rethinking Schools* booklet, *Selling Out Our Schools: Vouchers, Markets, and the Future of Public Education.*)

Throughout the book, the authors link market forces, the "new institution of public education," and the need for entrepreneurship among teachers. They correctly criticize unions for "propping up dysfunctional school systems" and rightfully advocate for more decision-making at the school level. But they appear willing to dismantle necessary centralized functions

and accountability. Their vision of schools is so decentralized that the dominant power in education becomes marketplace forces — which honor individual decision-making over collective democracy and which have always promoted the interests of children and families who have the money to seek out the best neighborhoods, schools, and educational services.

I believe that teacher unions can more effectively fight voucher and privatization schemes — and recalcitrant school boards — if they embrace educational innovation and flexibility. But Kerchner *et al.* seem to view innovation and flexibility as ways to make a market-based public school system more palatable.

What About Social Justice?

The authors' willingness to accept a market-based ideology of school reform is linked to an even more fundamental weakness in the book — the lack of analysis of schools' relationship to broader social issues. True, the authors talk about the future of schools in what they term a "knowledge society." But they ignore social issues of class, race, and gender inequalities. Without a broader social analysis, it's hard to talk about whether reforms such as charter schools, National Teacher Certification, or National Standards will promote equitable and quality schooling for all children.

The authors delineate between old-style unionism, which concentrates on "industrial" issues such as wages and working conditions, and a new unionism that organizes around "mental" issues such as quality teaching and education reform (don't forget, the book is titled *United Mind Workers*). Some traditional union activists are critical of the idea that "industrial" unionism is passé. They argue that given the "management" mentality of school boards and the anti-worker policies of many state governments, teacher unions need to keep a focus on "industrial" issues and tactics. I agree. But if teacher unions also adopt more "professional" stances — which at times conflict with traditional "industrial" concerns such as seniority — we will strengthen our ability to fight those forces who unrelentingly attack teachers and our system of public education.

Kerchner *et al.* help sharpen the debate around "industrial" versus "professional" unionism. But it is disappointing that the authors fail to recognize that teachers must also organize around "social" issues such as race and class inequity — a concept I call "social justice unionism." *United Mind Workers* is not completely oblivious to the connection between the broader social world and the conditions of learning and teaching. In the closing paragraphs of the book, the authors hint at the role teachers can play in social issues. "Teachers are in a position to advocate for children and to assist parents and families in building safe, decent communities," they note. They also write that "teachers, in greater numbers to a greater extent than any other adults, spend time with the nation's children," and that "unions can effectively advocate for children and can ... lead in recreating a politics of justice, tolerance, and kindness."

The problem is that in their entire 212-page book, this is all they have to say about social issues. Despite the huge impact on schools of problems such as poverty, discrimination, substance abuse, and jobless-ness, the authors are silent on how unions might help build a more just and equal society. One could read *United Mind Workers* and come away with the idea that all that is needed to transform American schools is for teacher unions to reorganize themselves on more professional lines.

The authors make important suggestions. But such proposals will not lead to quality education for all children unless they are linked to a commit-ment from teacher unions to work for social justice at the local, state, and national level.

It is unfortunate that the authors don't mention any efforts — either historical or current — of unionists advocating social justice or unions building coalitions with community forces to improve social conditions. The history of AFT Local 5 in the latter half of the 1930s is one example. Working in Harlem, the union collaborated with local community, parent, and church groups. The collaboration succeeded in getting two new schools built, in removing racist textbooks, and in promoting the study of African-American history and culture (see article, p. 86).

Granted, such examples are not common. But that's related to one of the main points I want to make. If teacher unions are truly concerned with safeguarding their members' rights and preserving our system of public schools, they must take up policies that pro-mote social justice. It is not just urban schools that are in crisis in this country. Our urban centers themselves are at risk. In response, most politicians advocate the building of more prisons, beefing up police forces, carving out "safe" neighborhoods for the middle class, and privileging urban development focused on sports

stadiums, corporate office space, and arts facilities. Rather than ignoring such realities, teacher unions should be in the forefront of demanding social policies that provide more resources for our children, families, and schools, particularly in urban areas.

Ignoring Race

In failing to take up social issues, the authors commit an even more egregious error: They don't deal with race. It's hard to believe that a book on education published in 1997 could ignore this issue. There are any number of important educational matters related to race — affirmative action, the decreasing number of students of color in teacher training institutions, the racial gap in achievement scores, problems with teacher expectations of students, and the increasingly white teaching force in urban schools that are increas-ingly populated by students of color. Indeed, it is no exaggeration to say that race is central to the future of schooling in this country. Neither classroom teachers, nor their organizations, can afford to remain silent on this matter.

By failing to under-score issues of race, the book foregoes any critical analysis and makes it impossible to highlight positive examples of how some unions have dealt with race and diversity — such as the British Columbia Teacher's Federation's anti-racist initiative (see article, p. 52).

Despite its shortcomings, however, *United Mind Workers* is sure to spark much-needed debate on the future of teacher unionism. In particular, it should foster discussion of professional issues that have too long been ignored in some union circles. Its shortcom-ings should not deter people from reading the book. My hope is that people go beyond the authors' analysis and wrestle with how the NEA and the AFT can embrace "social justice unionism" as a way to trans-form public education and preserve its democratic spirit. TTU

> *The authors commit an even more egregious error: They don't deal with race. It's hard to believe that a book on education published in 1997 could ignore this issue.*

Bob Peterson (RepMilw@aol.com) is an editor of *Rethinking Schools*, teaches Fifth Grade in Milwaukee, and is active in the Milwaukee Teachers Education Association.

This article originally appeared in the summer 1998 issue (Vol. 11, No. 4) of *Rethinking Schools*.

Social Justice Unionism: A Working Draft

The following statement was issued by 29 teacher-union activists following a three-day institute in Portland, Oregon, in August, 1994, sponsored by the National Coalition of Education Activists.

PUBLIC EDUCATION IS AT A CROSSROADS AND SO, too, are our unions. Our society's children face deepening poverty and social dislocation. Our schools face a growing crisis of confidence as they confront greater challenges and higher expectations with declining resources. Our unions face powerful political opponents, the punishing consequences of economic hard times, and a crisis of identity borne, in part, of uncertainty about our capacity to rise to the demands of the day.

As the organized core of the teaching profession, education unions remain central to resolving these crises. While there is some promising movement in new directions, the prospects for the future are far from certain.

Much is at stake. The rights of education workers and the interests of public education are under attack and must be defended and strengthened. But relying on strategies which in the past secured better lives for our members is no longer enough.

Economic hard times pose a sustained threat to hopes for improvement in the social welfare. Savage inequalities in the public education available to children of different racial and class backgrounds reflect growing social and economic polarization and squander the potential of our youth. Gaps between schools and the communities they serve are widening. The price of continued decay in public education and social well-being will be paid in reduced prospects for a democratic future.

With the stakes so high for ourselves and for our country, we have good reason to respond urgently to calls for reform. Yet too often that response has been reactive and timid. While some bold innovations have shown that union initiative can make a crucial difference, those initiatives have been the exception rather than the rule. Too often, unions have resisted reform efforts or have uncritically followed the lead of others, rather than raising the voices of educators and school communities. Too rarely does reform constructively affect our classrooms or our schools, with teachers and educators leading the way. Too many have been quick to blame children and their communities for school failure, and slow to identify educational policies and classroom practices that, in the long run, serve those who want to see public schools die out or be sold off to the highest bidder.

Prevailing definitions of educational success and failure remain overly preoccupied with standardized test scores or focused on narrow conceptions of economic competitiveness. Instead, reform should be driven by standards of equity and social justice, including high expectations and educational excellence for all. The ideals that led us to organize our unions and fight for economic justice — indeed, that led many of us to enter teaching in the first place — are no less compelling than in the past: a desire to help children; hope for the future; service to community; and a conviction that public education is a cornerstone of society's commitment to opportunity, equity, and democratic participation. But these ideals cannot be served by business-as-usual in our schools or in our unions. Both demand new vision.

Without a broader conception of the interests of teachers and of teaching, our unions will find themselves on ever-more shaky ground, defending fewer jobs and shrinking privileges against repeated attacks. Without a better partnership with the parents and communities that need public education most, we will find ourselves isolated from essential allies. Without a new vision of schooling that raises the expectations of our students and the standards of our own profession, we will continue to founder. Without a new model of unionism that revives debate and democracy internally and projects an inspiring social vision and agenda externally, we will fall short of the challenges before us.

Key Components of Social Justice Unionism

Social justice unionism retains the best of traditional unionism, borrows from what has been called "professional unionism," and is informed by a broader concept of our members' self-interests and by a deeper social vision. Social justice unionism should:

1. Defend the rights of its members while fighting for the rights and needs of the broader community and students.

The interests of education workers are best served by defending public education while simultaneously working to transform it. Unions of education workers need to accept some responsibility for the problems in public schools. We need to use our resources, membership, and power at the bargaining table and in the legislative arena to help resolve these problems.

For example, education unions should fight to extend collective bargaining laws to the 16 states that currently lack them, so that unions can better protect teachers and teaching. Yet they also need to be willing to reconsider contract language that proves to be an

obstacle to school reform.

2. Recognize that the parents and neighbors of our students are key allies, and build strategic alliances with parents, labor unions, and community groups.

Instead of promoting policies that may alienate the communities where our students live, we should forge alliances and resolve differences whenever possible.

Because parents play a central role in the education of their children and are our strongest political allies, education unions should work to insure that parents are full partners in our schools. Unions should advocate for significant parent and community involvement on local school governing bodies, and should urge staff to promote parental involvement in school activities. Where racial and cultural differences exist between our members and the communities they serve, the union should work pro-actively to close the gap. For example, unions should urge schools to communicate to the parents in their native language, to secure childcare and transportation for meetings and conferences, and to schedule meetings at times and places accessible to parents. Unions should lobby for legislation which would allow parents paid time off from their jobs for conferences and school activities.

Education unions should also work to unite all staff members at a school. They should build ongoing alliances with a wide range of groups, from other public service unions to the broader labor movement, churches, community and social organizations, advocacy groups, and business and political groups that support public schools. Such alliances are necessary to defeat budget cutbacks, fight for adequate and equitable funding of public education paid for by progressive tax reforms, and advocate for comprehensive school reform. Our unions must also participate in alliances taking up other issues affecting our students, such as job programs, housing, health care, recreation, safety, and anti-violence and anti-racism initiatives.

3. Fully involve rank-and-file members in running the union and initiate widespread discussion on how education unions should respond to the crises in education and society.

Only by changing the culture of our unions will they become a force for changing the culture of our schools. Many local education unions need to move from a "service" model — where inactive members are passive recipients of services provided by the paid staff — to a model where a mobilized membership takes active responsibility for union affairs. Members often feel that their union is as distant from them as the school administration. Communication is too often one-way, with union newspapers and newsletters rarely seeking opinions or input. Some local and state apparatuses are dominated by cliques of individuals, making entry into union activities difficult for new members or rank-and-file activists. While democratic structures formally exist in virtually all education employee unions, such structures on their own do not ensure democratic practices or membership involvement. Bureaucratic styles and parliamentary obstacles can too easily thwart a concerned member. Unions need to constantly encourage membership involvement and mobilization.

4. Put teachers and others who work in classrooms at the center of school reform agendas, ensuring that they take ownership of reform initiatives.

Those who work in schools and classrooms on a daily basis are in the best position to implement and evaluate school reform initiatives. Unfortunately, unions have not ensured that the voices of these

---

Without a new model of unionism that revives debate and democracy internally and projects an inspiring social vision and agenda externally, we will fall short of the challenges before us.

---

educators are adequately heard. Unions need to allocate sufficient resources to promote reform initiatives and build grassroots support for them.

Just as we demand that school administrators empower staff to make educational policy decisions, union leaders must equip their members to make decisions at local school levels. This means being open to changes in contract language that inhibits reform, and committing resources to train members for active, decision-making roles at the school level. While the union has a responsibility to protect the rights of all its members, only by moving more decision-making power to the school site will there be enough initiative and expertise to make school reform successful. Such a transfer of the locus of power, if done properly with adequate training, could also bring historically disenfranchised union members back into our organizations.

5. Encourage those who work with children to use methods of instruction and curricula that will promote racial and gender equity, combat racism and prejudice,

encourage critical thinking about our society's problems, and nurture an active, reflective citizenry that is committed to real democracy and social and economic justice.

Too often, schools fail to challenge students intellectually, dull their creativity, and bore them to a point of alienation from learning. Moreover, the difference in achievement levels between children of color and their white counterparts is totally unacceptable. Education unions should work with communities of color to address this grave problem.

Unions need to give higher priority to classroom and school-based practices that promote better education and equity for all students. These include: changes in curricula that affirm a child's home language and culture while teaching English and respect for all cultures; practices that promote gender equity; teacher training in the reduction of prejudice, including homophobia; alternatives to tracking and ability grouping; and school restructuring. In addition to the inherent merits such practices have, parents and communities who see unions promoting reforms that better serve their children's needs are more likely to support schools and teachers.

6. Forcefully advocate for a radical restructuring of American education.

Daily life for teachers must be changed from one of isolation and over-extension with few standards and little accountability, to one of collaboration, reflection, high standards, and mutual accountability. For this to happen, schools must be radically restructured. Some of the components of this restructuring include: lower class sizes so students can establish more productive relationships with teachers; smaller schools; a substantial increase in collaborative planning and staff development time; peer mentoring and evaluation; new, more equitable forms of standards and performance assessment; faculty selection processes in which the staff and principal of a school have more power; sharply reduced bureaucracy at all levels; and the reintegration of administrators into classroom teaching on a regular basis. Unions should use their power at the bargaining table and in the legislative arena to fight for these measures.

7. Aggressively educate and mobilize its membership to fight for social justice in all areas of society.

Growing racial and class divisions are threatening not just our schools, but the very foundations of our society. Education unions, from the local to the national level, must address these divisions. Ultimately, such problems will only be adequately addressed by a massive social movement similar to the civil rights movement and the movement against the War in Vietnam. In the short term, however, much can be done — from creating classrooms that encourage students to critically reflect and act on social problems, to building coalitions that address specific social problems.

Education unions need to move beyond a crisis orientation and become part of ongoing, long-term coalitions. We must stress constant, grassroots education and organizing and not just sporadic media blitzes. We must lobby behind the scenes but not forego militant public actions when necessary. We need to build bridges to political leaders and parties, but not rely too heavily on them. We need to work with others to build a political movement that is independent of the Democratic and Republican parties and that focuses on the fight for social and economic justice.

A Call to Action

Social justice unionism cannot be implemented in a top-down fashion. Nor can it be just words on paper. It will require both enlightened leadership and rank-and-file mobilization.

It will mean learning to teach in new ways; restructuring local union activities in new ways; reaching out to different communities in new ways; and building alliances at both local and state levels. It will require the national unions, perhaps one merged national teachers union, to provide leadership to build a national movement for social and economic justice.

Classroom and Building Level

For classroom teachers, social justice unionism might mean changing their methods of teaching so that they draw on students' experiences; developing alternatives to

Social justice unionism cannot be implemented in a top-down fashion. Nor can it be just words on paper. It will require both enlightened leadership and rank-and-file mobilization.

tracking, ability grouping, and antiquated forms of assessment; and embracing anti-racist, anti-bias approaches. Teachers and other workers most concerned about educational reform should demand that their unions facilitate that reform.

At the building level, social justice unions would move beyond the role of "information pushers" whose main presence is newsletters stuffed into mailboxes, to an expanded role that helps develop the capacities of members to participate in school restructuring and all union activities. School-based union committees or chapters might promote staff development activities, encourage site-based governance that would allow staff and parent decision making at the school, and push for the creation of structures and the freeing up of time for collegial dialogue and support. Such union committees could help mobilize members to advocate for progressive perspectives within the union, and, when working in concert with parents, advocate for the school as a whole before the administration and school board.

JEAN-CLAUDE LEJEUNE

Local, Community, and State Level

Internally, members need to demand changes in union structures and policies, so that democratic discussion is encouraged, training programs are available on labor/management relationships, pedagogical matters, and reform issues, and so that newer teachers feel that the union is an important part of their school lives.

Externally, a social justice union should be a public advocate for the needs not only of school staffs, but of public education, school restructuring, and most importantly, of their students and their communities. Such advocacy ranges from political action and coalition building to membership education.

Given the increasingly difficult straits facing public education, building alliances on the local and state levels is particularly important. Unions should build ongoing relations with organizations and communities to fight for equitable and adequate funding for schools, progressive school reform, programs to increase the number of teachers of color, and social initiatives such as universal health care, progressive tax reform, housing, jobs programs, and so forth.

National Level

On the national level, the likely merger of the NEA and the AFT presents an historic opportunity. Such a merged union would have the potential to become one of the most powerful advocates for children and social justice in our nation.

It is crucial that members fight for a merged union that is more democratic, more concerned about equity, and more capable of building and leading a national social movement around key social issues.

In the immediate term, local, state, and national offices of the AFT and NEA should initiate widespread discussion of the need for social justice unionism. The national offices can seed social justice unionism projects at the local level by allocating staff time and resources, and can encourage such perspectives by orienting conferences and training sessions toward that theme. Moreover, world economic trends make clear that unions in the U.S. must work cooperatively with unions and other social justice organizations on an international basis.

Ultimately, the likelihood of this vision becoming a reality rests on the actions of the members of both the NEA and AFT. These members understand that their commitment to children will best be served not only by being high-quality teachers and support staff, but also by being social justice advocates in a society that so desperately needs equality and justice. We encourage all like-minded people to join us in this effort. **TTU**

THE UNION INSTITUTE WAS ATTENDED BY THE FOLLOWING UNION ACTIVISTS FROM THE AFT AND NEA, INCLUDING NATIONAL STAFF, STATE AND LOCAL OFFICERS, AND RANK-AND-FILE MEMBERS (ORGANIZATIONS ARE LISTED FOR IDENTIFICATION PURPOSES ONLY):

BARRY ABEL, LOCAL ASSISTANCE AND DEVELOPMENT, NEA
NINA BASCIA, FACULTY OF EDUCATION, UNIVERSITY OF TORONTO
SARA BELCHER-BARNES, UNITED FEDERATION OF TEACHERS BUILDING REPRESENTATIVE, P.S. 130, DISTRICT 15, NEW YORK CITY
ROSCOE CARON, EXECUTIVE BOARD, EUGENE EDUCATION ASSOCIATION
MICHAEL CHARNEY, EXECUTIVE BOARD, CLEVELAND TEACHERS' UNION
MAGGIE CRAIN, DIRECTOR OF PUBLICATIONS, SEATTLE EDUCATION ASSOCIATION
TOM EDMINSTER, BUILDING REPRESENTATIVE AND EXECUTIVE BOARD MEMBER, UNITED EDUCATORS OF SAN FRANCISCO (AFT/NEA)
JACKIE ELLENZ, PORTLAND ASSOCIATION OF TEACHERS
MARGARET GARRISON, REPRESENTATIVE, OLYMPIC UNISERV COUNCIL, WASHINGTON
DONNA GOLD, NATIONAL CENTER FOR INNOVATION, NEA
DARLA HARTLEY, FIELD ASSISTANT, OLYMPIC UNISERV COUNCIL, WASHINGTON
LYNDA HAYASHI, PARENT OUTREACH COORDINATOR, SPOKANE EDUCATION ASSOCIATION
JOEL JORDAN, UNITED TEACHERS-LOS ANGELES
STAN KARP, EXECUTIVE BOARD, PATERSON EDUCATION ASSOCIATION, PATERSON, NJ.
GRAINGER LEDBETTER, PRESIDENT, ARKANSAS EDUCATION ASSOCIATION
LARRY LEWIN, HUMAN AND CIVIL RIGHTS COMMITTEE, EUGENE EDUCATION ASSOCIATION
HEATHER LEWIS, DIRECTOR, CENTER FOR COLLABORATIVE EDUCATION, NEW YORK CITY
BARBARA McGREW, CENTER FOR MEMBERSHIP AND AFFILIATES, NEA
CORA McHENRY, EXECUTIVE DIRECTOR, ARKANSAS EDUCATION ASSOCIATION
TOM MOONEY, PRESIDENT, CINCINNATI FEDERATION OF TEACHERS
BOB PETERSON, MILWAUKEE TEACHERS EDUCATION ASSOCIATION, *RETHINKING SCHOOLS*
DIANA PORTER, CHAIR, EDUCATIONAL POLICIES COMMITTEE, CINCINNATI FEDERATION OF TEACHERS
DINA PORTNOY, PHILADELPHIA SCHOOLS COLLABORATIVE
ANN RANDALL, REPRESENTATIVE, OLYMPIC UNISERV COUNCIL, WASHINGTON
MARK SIMON, NEA BOARD OF DIRECTORS
KENT SPRING, SECRETARY, PORTLAND ASSOCIATION OF TEACHERS
RITA TENORIO, MILWAUKEE TEACHERS EDUCATION ASSOCIATION, *RETHINKING SCHOOLS*
BEN VISNICK, PRESIDENT, OAKLAND EDUCATION ASSOCIATION
HOWARD YANK, CO-CHAIR, HUMAN AND CIVIL RIGHTS COMMITTEE, EUGENE EDUCATION ASSOCIATION

FOR COPIES OF THIS DRAFT DOCUMENT, OR INFORMATION ABOUT ACTIVITIES TO PROMOTE THIS VISION OF SOCIAL JUSTICE UNIONISM, CONTACT NCEA, BOX 679, RHINEBECK, NY 12572; 914-876-4580.

Questions and Answers

BY BOB PETERSON

When people talk about "new unionism" what do they mean?

The phrase "new unionism" was popularized by NEA President Bob Chase when speaking before the National Press Club in February 1997. It's been most associated with the perspective that calls on unions to take responsibility for teacher quality — adopt a more professional, student-focused emphasis, and one that is more collaborative with local school authorities. Programs such as career ladders and peer mentoring and review are associated with "new unionism."

But doesn't collaboration between unions and management mean that the union is selling out its members? Doesn't this mimic corporate calls for "cooperation" and "quality circles"?

Actually unions collaborate with management all the time — every time they sign a contract. But we should collaborate on more than what's in the contract — in many places, state law prohibits bargaining on essential educational matters. When we do collaborate we should do so from positions of strength. The experience of the Cincinnati Federation of Teachers

JEAN-CLAUDE LEJEUNE

and the Rochester Teachers Association shows that by strongly advocating for educational reform, the union increases its strength and its ability to expand wages and benefits.

Labor and management in school districts have a common interest in students — which is different than a private company whose main concern is production and profits. Also keep in mind that local education authorities are quasi-democratic institutions, much different than corporations that make no pretense of being democratic. Teacher unions should work to ensure that local education authorities represent the interests of the vast majority of the population so that collaboration with such authorities can contribute to the overall improvement and preservation of public education.

In the Cleveland Teachers Union, every building chair gets time off — middle and high school teachers get a period off each day for union business, and all building reps get three days off during the year for leadership development.

Some "new unionism" promoters have criticized what they call the old "industrial model" of unionism. But isn't the problem really just with bureaucratic unions?

Bureaucracy is a serious problem in all organizations. Unions are not exempt. Some local teacher unions could definitely benefit from changes in their internal election and decision-making processes. Without strong democratic practices, the rank-and-file quickly become alienated from the union as a whole, weakening the union and the teaching profession in the process.

It's worth noting that compared to most other institutions in our society, teacher unions are relatively democratic. The debate around merger between the AFT and NEA is a case in point. There was widespread discussion and ultimately the delegates to the NEA convention voted against the NEA leadership's pro-merger position. Contrast that to how corporate America conducts their mergers of different companies — even though the consequences can affect tens of thousands of employees.

Let's grant that unions are more democratic than corporations — that's not saying much. But what about the problem of undemocratic unions?

It is a problem, particularly in some locals where a small group of people (either staff in NEA locals, or elected leadership in AFT locals) have constructed an insular group whose actions become self-serving. We are not saying that longevity in leadership is inherently undemocratic, just that in some cases in both the NEA and AFT, it has been. A social justice vision of unionism holds that elections should be democratic, that structures for rank-and-file discussion of important issues be established, and that decision-making include the membership.

Another way to look at this is to think of a "service union" versus an "organizing union." Many teacher unions have become good service providers — enforcing the contract, advising members on pensions and benefits, etc. Unfortunately along with this provision of service is an absence of a sense of the importance of organizing — the initial dynamic impulses of unionism that elicited broad participation by members. Now more than ever, teacher unions need an "organizing" mentality — not only organizing the unorganized education workers in charter schools and contracted service areas, but also organizing their own union members to militantly defend public education and to demand reform that will serve the needs of all children. Too often teachers think of the union as someone other than themselves — the staff or few elected officials in the union office.

So you are talking not only about democratic practices but increasing member participation. How can that be done?

Unions need to create specific structures to encourage teacher participation — providing when possible time, compensation, and other incentives. For example, in the Cleveland Teachers Union, every building chair gets time off — middle and high school teachers get a period off each day for union business, and all building reps get three days off during the year for leadership development. In Cincinnati, the union has negotiated an arrangement so that district-wide curriculum councils are led by lead teachers, providing a financial incentive for teachers to take a leadership role in such work. The bottom line: Formal democracy can become irrelevant if participation isn't forthcoming.

What's the difference between "social justice unionism" and "new unionism"?

Social justice unionism incorporates much of the new unionism perspective but does so through the lens of equity and social justice. The two perspectives are not antagonistic, although "new unionism" proponents at times are silent on how new union programs affect issues of equity for students. The social justice perspective holds that all teacher-union policies should be forged in such a way as to promote equity. Moreover, the social justice unionist perspective places a great importance on the need for a strategic alliance between parents and community groups that have been historically disenfranchised on one hand, and teacher unions and all of the labor movement on the other. In contrast, some new unionists tend to prioritize building alliances with business interests and corporations.

By saying you are for new unionism or social justice unionism, aren't you rejecting what was good about the old-fashioned industrial unionism that got teachers the rights that they enjoy now?

No. Most rights that teachers have now should be maintained or expanded. To build a strong public education system, we need teachers to have high salaries, good benefits, and secure working conditions. However, we also need teachers to take on the responsibility of ensuring quality in their profession. That may mean being innovative in matters such as school staffing policies, peer mentoring, and evaluation. We will actually be defending many of our basic rights if we take up the concerns of students and community, thereby improving and maintaining public education.

On the one hand, you are saying that we should be professionals — and yet also "class conscious," acting like regular workers? Isn't that contradictory?

It's non-traditional, but it's not contradictory. To be a "professional" doesn't mean one is not a worker. We sell our labor power, and get a paycheck. Just as many doctors are recognizing the need to organize themselves into unions, teachers have long recognized that without collective protection, they are subject to arbitrary decisions by administrators. But teachers need to stretch beyond even this "trade-union" perspective. Teachers need to take responsibility for the quality of the profession and recognize that student success is the ultimate goal. Success of students is the common bond between communities and teachers. Demanding that our unions adopt policies that promote such success is essential to both our individual and collective survival as teachers. Individually our jobs would be much more satisfying. Collectively we would garner greater political support from parents and communities. Ultimately we need to recognize that factors effecting the most disenfranchised seg-

ments of our community ultimately affect us all, and thus we should work for social justice in all areas of society.

Doesn't social justice unionism mean that we are just going to be supporting everybody else's struggle, which will ultimately just divide our union?

We mustn't underestimate the power of the conservative right and corporate elites in their attempts to dismantle the public sector and destroy teacher unions. If they get their way, there won't be much left of teacher unions to be "divided." The key to our defense is to make sure that the public sector provides the best services possible. To do this we need to forge a historic alliance with broad sectors of the general population — parents, community groups, religious leaders, and citizens who are concerned with the welfare of the entire society.

We do this primarily by taking up issues of equity

and justice in our schools. These issues include smaller class sizes, before- and after-school programs, mechanisms to ensure that all teachers are qualified and have time for periodic staff development, and policies that ensure that all students are being treated and taught equitably.

But even promoting these "social justice" education issues is not enough. The most profound factor affecting student achievement is the socio-economic status of the student's family. If we are serious about ensuring equity and success for all our students, then we need to join with other forces to demand equity and justice for *all members of society* in economic, social, and political arenas of our nation.

This is essential for two reasons. First, because it is best for kids. They all deserve equity and justice in school and outside of it. Second, it is the only way we can fight the enemies of public education. To do anything less is to set ourselves up for failure. Here's the problem: Some educational reformers and union leaders claim that there will be "success for all" if only schools are provided with adequate resources and programming. Yet given the social and economic conditions of our kids, some of them most likely won't be able to succeed even under vastly improved school conditions. When this occurs, the political right will claim that the extra funding for schooling was a waste,

that the public schools are inherently incapable of providing student success.

Does this mean we give up on these kids or not advocate for far-reaching education reforms? Of course not. But it does mean that teacher unions need to make clear, by their statements and actions, that they know that school success will only come if we simultaneously transform both our schools and society into more just and equitable places.

For this reason, it is important to support struggles in areas of health care, housing, jobs, and ending discrimination. By doing so, we build allies for our efforts to transform schools and we improve the quality of life in our communities, which benefits both students and ourselves.

When a union takes up controversial issues, there will be differences among members. That's okay, and in fact is a sign of life for an organization. If debate and discussion are democratic, and members are well-informed politically, most potential problems of "division" can be averted. The rights of the minority should be protected, but not allowed to paralyze the will of the majority. Debate and study around such issues will breathe life into our unions, and hopefully inspire many more teachers to recognize that it is in their self-interest to insist that their unions promote social justice. TTU

Resources
and Study Guide

Resources

Organizations: Teacher Unions and Education

American Federation of Teachers, 555 New Jersey Ave., NW, Washington, DC 20001. 202-879-4400. Internet: www.aft.org. Publishes *American Teacher*.

National Education Association, 1201 16th St., NW, Washington, DC 20036-3290. 202-833-4000. Internet: www.nea.org. Publishes *NEA Today*. To see examples of "new unionism," connect to www.nea.org/newunion/.

National Coalition of Education Activists, PO Box 679, Rhinebeck, NY 12572. 914-876-4580, or email rfbs@aol.com. A network of parent, teacher, and community activists focused on organizing for equity and school reform. Publishes the newsletter, *Action for Better Schools*. Internet: http://members.aol.com/nceaweb.

National Commission on Teaching and America's Future, Box 117, Teachers College, Columbia University, 525 West 120th St., New York, NY 10027. Fax: 212-678-4039; Internet: www.tc.columbia.edu/~teachcomm/. While this commission doesn't explicitly deal with union reform, their proposals to change the status of teachers warrant consideration. In particular, check out their booklet, *Doing What Matters Most: Investing in Quality Teaching*, November, 1997.

Rethinking Schools, 1001 E. Keefe Ave., Milwaukee, WI 53212. 800-669-4192; fax: 414-964-7220. Internet: www.rethinkingschools.org. Publishes the quarterly *Rethinking Schools* and various books. Regularly reports on union reform issues. Free catalog available.

Teachers Union Reform Network of AFT-NEA Locals (TURN), c/o Rochester Teachers Association, 30 N. Union St., Suite 301, Rochester, New York

14607. 716-546-2681; fax: 716-546-4123; email: urbanski@servtech.com. Internet: www.turnexchange.net. A coalition of NEA and AFT locals whose leaders meet to exchange ideas on innovative educational reform. Their website has links to all participating locals and examples of contract language organized by reform topics: shared decision-making, peer assistance and evaluation, staff development, parent involvement/engagement, alternative compensation and charter/pilot schools. To see contract language, go to: www.turnexchange.net/contracts/contract-matrix.htm

Other Organizations

American Federation of Labor - Congress of Industrial Organizations (AFL-CIO), 815 16th St. NW, Washington, DC 20006. 800-342-1235. Internet: www.aflcio.org. The Education Department and Policy Department have useful information.

KATHY SLOANE

Labor Notes, a monthly newsletter of news and analysis about ongoing labor union and rank-and-file activities. ($20/year). Published by Labor Education and Research Project, 7435 Michigan Ave., Detroit, MI 48210. 313-842-6262; Internet: www.labornotes.org.

Network of Educators on the Americas (NECA). PO Box 73038, Washington, DC 20056. 202-238-2379; email: necadc@aol.com; Internet: www.teachingforchange.org. A comprehensive collection of multicultural and social-justice curricular and resource materials, including labor history. Ask for the free "Teaching for Change" catalog.

Trinational Coalition in Defense of Public Education. Canada, United States, and Mexico. PO Box 602, Olympia, WA 98507. 360-866-6000, Ext. 6478; email: sanpatricio@igc.org. A coalition of teacher unions working to build understanding of the public-school and union systems in order to coordinate joint actions to preserve public education as a social right.

Books: Historical Perspectives on U.S. Teacher Unionism

Markowitz, Ruth Jacknow. *My Daughter, The Teacher: Jewish Teachers in the New York City Schools.* New Brunswick, NJ: Rutgers University Press, 1993. A detailed account of many socially-committed teachers and their union activities in the first half of the 1900s.

Murphy, Marjorie. *Blackboard Unions: The AFT and the NEA 1900-1980.* Ithaca, NY: Cornell University Press, 1990. An overview of eight decades of teacher-union activities and politics.

Zitron, Celia Lewis. *The New York City Teachers Union, 1916-1964.* New York: Humanities Press, 1968. The most definitive work on the history of the union with special emphasis on its educational and social policies.

Books: Teacher Unions and School Reform

Kerchner, C. and Julia Koppich. *A Union of Professionals: Labor Relations and Educational Reform.* New York: Teachers College Press, 1993. An examination of professional unionism through several case studies.

Kerchner, C., Julia E. Koppich and Joseph G. Weeres. *United Mind Workers: Unions and Teaching in the Knowledge Society.* San Francisco: Jossey-Bass, 1997. A perspective on professional unionism and its contractual and legislative implications. (See review, p. 123.)

Peer Assistance Peer Review: An AFT/NEA Handbook. Washington, DC: NEA and AFT, 1998. Available from Gina Carmon at the Teaching and Learning Unit, NEA. 202-822-7355; fax: 202-822-7482; email: GCarmon@NEA.org.

Facilitating the Dialogue on Peer Assistance and Peer Review, by NEA. Washington, DC: NEA, 1998. Available from Kelly Cedeno, Training and Organization Development, NEA. 202-822-7183; fax: 202-822-7168.

Stepping Forward: How NEA Members Are Revitalizing America's Public Schools, by the NEA. Washington DC: NEA, 1999. Available from NEA Communications, 202-822-7200.

Books: International Perspectives

Barber, Michael. *Education and The Teachers Unions.* London: Cassell, 1992. A concise history of the National Teachers Union of England and Wales with an examination of issues surrounding professionalism and school reform.

Cook, Maria Lorena. *Organizing Dissent: Unions, the State and the Democratic Teachers' Movement in Mexico.* University Park, PA: Pennsylvania State University Press, 1996. An examination of the democratic movement within the National Union of Education Workers, the largest union of Latin America.

Lawn, Martin, ed. *The Politics of Teacher Unionism: International Perspectives.* London: Croom Helm, 1985. Essays on the politics of teacher unions in several European and Asian countries.

Robertson, Susan and Harry Smaller. *Teacher Activism in the 1990s.* Toronto: Our Schools/Our Selves, 1996. A collection of essays that examine the multiple roles teacher unions have played in Canada. To order, call 800-565-1975, or 416-463-6978. ⊞

Questions for Discussion

BY BOB PETERSON AND MICHAEL CHARNEY

The following questions may be helpful to facilitate discussions among educators who read this book. We welcome feedback on the book as well as suggestions on how to conduct discussions around these important topics.

1. There will be a need for hundreds of thousands of new teachers in the next five years. Many will have little understanding of the history of labor or teacher unions. In what ways can teacher unions use their resources and staff to pass on the history of teacher unions? What are the salient themes new teachers need to know? What are some of the candid weaknesses of teacher unions they need to know?

2. In the Introduction, social justice unionism is described as having three components. In what ways do these three components intersect? To what extent are they mutually exclusive? What are the obstacles for implementing a coherent direction for teacher unionism in your local or state organization?

3. Recently some locals have adopted peer review programs to assist and, if necessary, to remove under-performing teachers. What are the contradictions of implementing such a program? What are the advantages? What can advocates of peer review do to win support among union members and the public at large? (See articles on Rochester, Cincinnati, and Minneapolis, beginning on pp. 33, 40, and 46 respectively.)

4. The British Columbia Teachers' Federation set up a comprehensive program to deal with racism in the schools (see article, p. 52). What opportunities exist for a teachers union to explicitly develop an anti-racism program for children and its own members? What are ways a union wins support for such a potentially controversial approach? How can a union balance its resources to negotiate a contract, engage in political action, service its members, and oversee an anti-racism project?

5. Margaret Haley, the Chicago union leader in the early 1900s, argued, "There is no possible conflict between the interests of the child and the interests of the teacher .... For both the child and the teacher, freedom is the condition of development." (See article, p. 78.) Do you think this is true? How should unions handle potential conflicts between member interests and those of children or parents? How does a union determine member, parent, and child interests?

6. Can a teacher union consisting of many different viewpoints and racial and ethnic backgrounds take up the issue of race? Should it? In what ways can a teachers union gain community support by downplaying racial inequity? In what ways can a teacher union gain community support by organizing against inequity? (For historical examples, see articles by Kohl, p. 93, and Perlstein, p. 86, on teacher-union struggles in New York.)

7. How important is internal democracy in a teachers union for improving the life of its members? For improving public schools? The NEA Representative Assembly operates on a secret ballot, while the AFT convention has an open ballot. Defenders of each position claim their view is democratic. What are the advantages and disadvantages of each position? How can union democracy and membership participation be improved on the local level? (See Bastian's "What Happened to the NEA/AFT Merger?" p. 99, and the NCEA statement, p. 128.)

8. The public sector is larger than public education. They are both under attack. In the interview with Bill Fletcher (p. 117) and the excerpt from NEA President Bob Chase (p. 120), each describes the vital role the public sector plays and how it must be defended. How can we simultaneously defend the public sector while demanding it be improved? What sections of the public sector should be strengthened in your community and how might that be done?

9. Howard Zinn states in his interview (p. 73) that "If teacher unions want to be strong and well-supported, it's essential that they not only be teacher unionists but teachers of unionism. We need to create a generation of students who support teachers and the movement of teachers for their rights." What efforts does your teachers union make to help teachers become more effective in teaching about union history and social protest? How might your union, other unions, and concerned citizens promote such teaching and learning? **TTU**

FOR OTHER ARTICLES ON TEACHER UNIONISM AND CRITICISM AND FEEDBACK ON THIS BOOK, CHECK OUT THE WEBSITE OF RETHINKING SCHOOLS AT: WWW.RETHINKINGSCHOOLS.ORG.

PLEASE CONTACT THE EDITORS OF THIS BOOK WITH YOUR FEEDBACK AND IDEAS. LETTERS ADDRESSED TO *RETHINKING SCHOOLS* WILL BE CONSIDERED FOR PUBLICATION IN THE QUARTERLY JOURNAL. TO CONTACT THE EDITORS DIRECTLY:

BOB PETERSON: RFPMILW@AOL.COM
MICHAEL CHARNEY: MICHAELCTU@AOL.COM

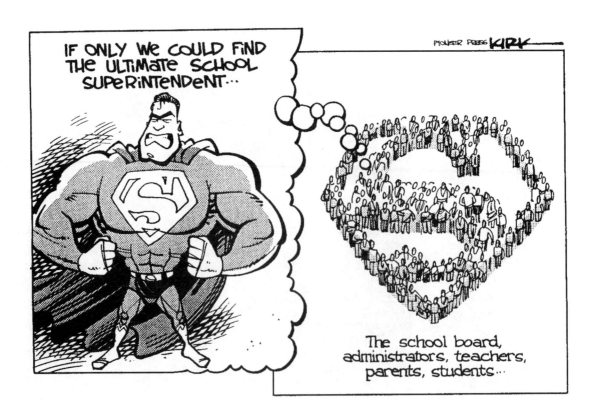

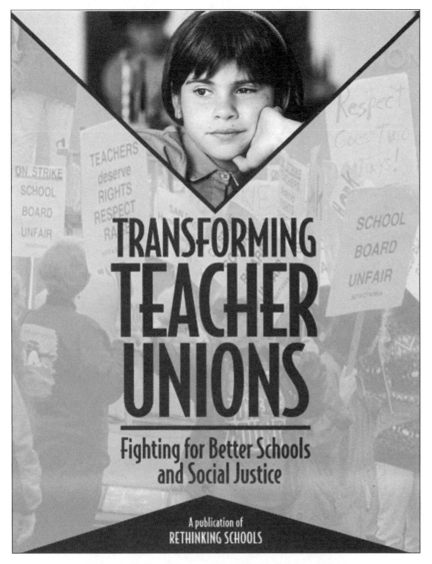